Business Lessons from Hollywood

What I Learned as an Entrepreneur in the Capital of Entertainment

by Atom Alex Helling

BUSINESS LESSONS FROM HOLLYWOOD:
What I Learned As An Entrepreneur in the Capital of Entertainment

ISBN: 150230094X

ISBN-13: 978-1502300942

DEDICATION

To my friends and foes in Hollywood.

I thank you for the valuable lessons you taught me in life and business.

CONTENTS

INTRODUCTION: DOING BUSINESS HOLLYWOOD-STYLE

Have you ever been to Hollywood? Even if you have not, you know that it is much more than a small district in central Los Angeles. It is a figure of speech for the motion picture industry of the United States, a magic word that evokes colorful associations, some glamorous, others less so. Its impact reaches far beyond language barriers. Every blockbuster was either produced in the city or relied on its talent at some stage for "that Hollywood look." Most TV shows that flicker across screens worldwide have their origins there. So do pop songs, computer games, fashion and lifestyle trends. The hold of Hollywood on global entertainment is a fact. Debating whether this is a good thing is outside the scope of this book. Nevertheless, if one thing is clear, then it is that to become Hollywood, more than some good connections and serendipity are necessary. More than anything else, it demands a different set of business skills.

What Would Hollywood Do?

Do you sometimes wonder how movie producers, directors, film stars, musicians, and other celebrities run their business affairs? Their aspirations often go beyond their on-screen personas. Next to decorating the covers of magazines, these people have businesses to run. Restaurants, apparel, and endorsement deals are a staple with most celebrities. Many of them are surprisingly adept at running real estate firms, venture capital funds, and other endeavors that demand a keen business sense. Being Hollywood, they naturally do things a little different. And that stretches far beyond the entertainment industry. All business in Los Angeles follows its own rules. From the barista/screenwriter, to the studio executive, the law firm, the car dealership, all the way to the dry cleaner, the city has a distinct style when it comes to doing business.

When I moved from the backwater to Los Angeles, I had to quickly learn the ropes of this new world. Over the next seven years, I would start several companies as an entrepreneur there. The business lessons in this book are a direct result of that. They all build on my personal adventures, good and bad. Some of them are more obvious, others go well beyond what you may find in the management literature. There are other ways to run a business, of course. The lessons in this book just give you an impression how Hollywood – as I see it – would do it. It will offer you suggestions to tackle situations from a fresh angle.

What This Book Is About

There is plenty of advice about breaking into the entertainment business. How to make it big in the movies is of little concern in this book. Even though Hollywood follows its own set of rules, it is still all about *business*. As expected, everything needs to be larger than life. Even the management strategies it requires are several notches bigger, brighter, and louder than in more conventional lines of work. If you are interested in learning how successful companies and individuals compete in the shark tank that is Hollywood, then this book is for you. Consider it your unfair advantage over those following more conventional guidelines.

There is no other place on earth like Hollywood, and my experiences there were unique. After moving away from California, it surprised me when I realized how well some of them translated into my current projects outside of the entertainment industry. Perhaps the distance made it easier to see the connections. In retrospect, this place taught me invaluable lessons in business and in life.

Wherever in the world you live, you will learn something new by reading this book. Along the way, we have some fun, too. Feel free to shake your head at some of my blunders, and find out what learned from them. I apply the business lessons I picked up in Hollywood every day. I hope some of them will be inspiring for you as well.

Atom Alex Helling
Hong Kong, September 2014

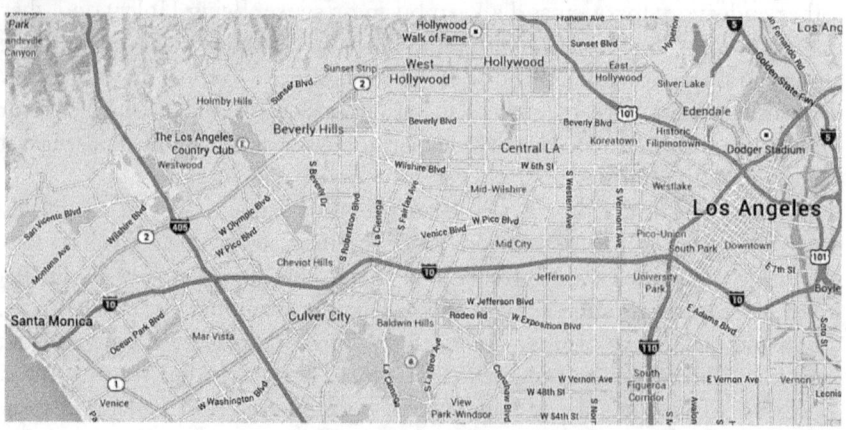

Map of Los Angeles with Santa Monica, Venice, Culver City, Central L.A.,
Beverly Hills, West Hollywood, Hollywood, and Downtown (image credit: Google)

CHAPTER 1: HOW TO ESTABLISH YOURSELF

I will always remember when I started my first business in Los Angeles. I had just moved to a new office in Venice Beach, across the road from the infamous Gold's Gym, with the goal to open a recording studio. I would compose film music, perhaps even become the next platinum producer. Of course, things took a different turn, as they always do. I managed to score some films and produce some records, but I learned that there were other people much more talented than me. So I ventured out and produced a documentary film. After all, I reasoned, being in Hollywood, I should produce at least one film. I also founded a think thank, a Japanese content production company, and a software company. And I consulted clients on their business ventures. But this chapter is about something else. What we are interested in here is how to go about starting a new project from scratch. Whenever you do that, you need to establish yourself in a new environment, with a new set of supporters, and new clients. Let's find out how to do this, Hollywood-style.

Just Do It

To launch a business in Hollywood, the best approach is to just do it. It is as simple as that. When I asked my accountant if I had to register my first company, incorporate it as a legal entity, and alert the tax authorities, he laughed. "On your next tax return, we just say you're a sole proprietor, and that's it. You'll save a lot of taxes that way." But what about the proper paperwork and filing the right forms? "Forget about it. If they want you to do that, then let them find you and make you do it." My friends told me the same thing. The costs for phone lines, broadband Internet, bank accounts, and insurance would be much higher for a business than for a private entity, with the service being be exactly the same. "Stay private as long as you can," they advocated.

So for tax purposes, I was a business. Everything else was for personal use. My first company remained unregistered for a long time, without any negative consequences. When I later started companies together with other founders, I registered them as corporations or limited liability companies (LLCs). Nevertheless, I saved much paperwork on my private, smaller ventures.

Years later I discovered that there was in fact a process to set up a sole proprietorship. An elderly lady from the city rang the doorbell of my office and asked if I was performing a business activity on the premises. Naïve as I was, I truthfully responded. Her eyes lit up. "Well, if that's the case, you will need a business license, which costs 500 dollars per year." I could have just as well answered that I was just pursuing my hobby in that office, or that the principal was on vacation in Hawaii. She would have probably just moved on to the next tenant with her fishing expedition. From that day, it became more difficult to fly below the radar.

Business Lesson

Instead of worrying about rules and regulations in your new ventures, just do it. If there is a problem, somebody will sooner or later tell you.

Team Up With Those More Successful Than You

I know almost nobody when I moved to Hollywood, so I needed to build most of my contacts from scratch. To do this, we usually all go for the lowest-hanging fruit first. Candidates are the club of expats that already lives in the city, or professional associations. Slowly they expand and find new avenues where they can meet potential business partners and clients.

I was exactly the same. In the first few weeks, I tried to meet with as many of my fellow countrymen as I could. I joined all professional organizations for music composers and went to their networking events. Being new to Hollywood, it was interesting for a while to see new faces and drive out to new places. But then it slowly dawned on me that everyone I was hanging out with was exactly in the same boat as me. Most of them had moved to the city recently and started to get their feet wet. None them had landed interesting work or had any experience besides the general knowledge one could read in a book. Those with exciting projects who were actually successful had no time and interest to stand around in some movie theater lobby and eat party dip from Costco. As soon as I landed my first projects, this set of people became jealous. It was only when I broke away from that early group of acquaintances that good things started happening for me.

Networking takes an effort, so you may as well make it count. It takes the same amount of energy to meet someone without the ability to help you and someone who could change your life for the better. You should target high-powered relationships right from the start. How to do this, you ask? Just think about your potential clients and where they go. Which clubs do they visit, which sports to they do? What do they read? Then do the same thing and get yourself in front of them as much as possible. This is an excellent filter for invitations to events. Just ask yourself if your clients or other successful people in your field would attend. If that is unlikely, then politely decline.

Successful people are more likely to give you honest advice how to do things right. If you are new in town, forget about trying to bond with other newbies and move up the ladder quick. The same applies to those in the same field as you. Better look for a diverse network with a minimum of competition within the group, where you can actually help each other in your projects. Opportunism is your friend, it is what you need to build a strong network in Hollywood.

Business Lesson

Build a network with successful people right from the start. Make contact with potential clients and those who are ahead of you. They influence you positively and will help you become one of them.

Look and Story Are Everything

Hollywood loves a good story. After all, the entire town only exists because it mastered the craft of turning even the most banal events into a gripping plot. You can recount most blockbuster movies in one sentence. Titanic: "A guy and a girl fall in love on an ill-fated ocean voyage that ends in the tragic death of the male protagonist." Transformers: "Alien robots that can shift their shape into cars wreak havoc on earth when they fight rebels from outer space." You get the point. The whole synopsis needs to come across in as few words as possible. Unless you can do that, your story needs work.

When I produced pop music in Los Angeles, I learned about the power of story. I had always thought that the most important thing was the emotional quality of the music. The lyrics, and the instrumentation, let alone their masterful arrangement, and the balanced mix. How wrong was I. In Hollywood, the main assets of a music project are the *look* and the *story*. You can always buy the rest somewhere else. But when the project lacks these two core ingredients, you have nothing.

It should be clear what I mean with "look." You need appealing faces and bodies. Whether they are the best singers available is absolutely unimportant. That is where technology comes in. Even famous singers sound underwhelming without post-processing of their vocal takes. The "story" sums up what the project is all about. This often boils down to the history of the singer, how he or she got into music, her trials and tribulations, and what the lyrics express. If you are working with a band, each member needs an identity. The guitar player is the bad guy, the girl on

9

the drums is dentist turned tattoo artist, and so on. Mind you, none of this needs to be true. In fact, most of these stories have their roots in caffeine-fueled brainstorming sessions.

Now comes the important part: The stories and identities you created need to come across visually for immediate impact. If you portray someone as a bad guy, have him wear black clothes and dim the lights in the photo shoot. Write his name in letters that look like knives. If your music has Brazilian elements in it, then you dress people up like Brazilian soccer players or have them pose on the beach as dancers. This focus on the story works outside the entertainment industry as well. Tell the benefits of your product or service in few words and then translate it with pictures and graphic design. Make sure everything in your presentation is compatible. If you rely on data that is hard to wrap into good story and visual representation, then find other attributes. Can you explain every font or color in your presentation? You have arrived in Hollywood.

Business Lesson

You need a strong visual story to convince others. This may be an investment thesis, or a rationale why a company is better than a competitor. Tell the story with images and design. Every font and color should fit.

Do Something Old With a Twist

When you start a business or a project in Hollywood, always understand its *angle*. Now what do I mean by that? I am talking about how your project fits into the landscape of existing material. Other projects of a film studio, the latest blockbusters, or the music in the charts, for example. When you speak about your ideas, explain them relative to what is already out there. Directors and writers often pitch their projects with something like "think Scarface meets Godzilla," or "imagine X-Men but with zoo animals." They mash their ideas with others that exists already. For this to work, their new ideas must overlap with existing ones in one way or another. Otherwise, the decision makers with the power to green light their projects will have a hard time to know what to make of them. The same goes for mainstream audiences. When a movie or song is already vaguely familiar, it will be much easier to understand.

You may feel you want to break new ground, and do something entirely new. This is the wrong strategy in Hollywood. Better find something that is already there and then use it as the setting for your own project. A music venture of mine with a Japanese singer became unexpectedly successful. All the lyrics were in Japanese, but the beats and melodies were similar to other female hip-hop artists at the time. I believe the music resonated with audiences in America because they could connect with a style that they already knew. The twist was in the Japanese lyrics. Had we tried to do something artsy or entirely new, I doubt we would have gotten that far. The irony is that record label executives commented how "new" they felt the music was. However, the only thing new was that the lyrics of the song were in an exotic language.

When you add a small twist, the whole product takes on a new shine. It alters perception. To be successful, better let others be the true pioneers. Then build on their work and add a twist. This is the recipe of success that Hollywood has followed for decades.

Business Lesson

Instead of introducing radically new ideas, better build on something that already exists and add a twist. This is easier to pitch to decision makers, and your target audience will know what to expect.

Have More Than One Idea to Pitch

After I had composed my first film scores and started to write pop songs, I felt that I needed to open up my studio to other producers as well. Especially when making music for TV commercials, it is common that several composers band together as a so-called "music house." They work on projects as a team and hope to become more successful this way. But how does one find new talent in Hollywood? Craigslist, the infamous free marketplace and job fair is a treasure trove for situations like these. When I placed an ad there, it took but a few days until literally hundreds of show reels from composers poured in. I was onto something, I felt, and started sifting through the material to find suitable candidates.

At the same time, a friend of mine who had successfully invested in Internet companies, was looking for a new entertainment venture to support. Together with a business partner he had started a seed-stage venture capital firm, and he believed that the music house may be a candidate for their portfolio. When we were meeting for coffee, he told me about his plans and invited me to present to the other partner. "Who knows," he said, "if he likes your idea, we might invest." A week later I drove up to their office with a pitch I had put together, ready to pick up a check.

The two men politely listened and nodded, when about ten minutes into the pitch, the other partner interjected, "You know, this is all fine and well, but we're trying to stay away from service businesses. Do you have anything else?" I thought hard for a few seconds, but nothing came to mind on the fly. As a result, the meeting fizzled out. On the drive home a variety of product ideas came to my mind. I should have thought about those earlier on. Who knows if that could have saved me and landed investment from the venture capital firm. But I had missed out on a chance to make the best impression. In Hollywood, some situations never return. I showed up with more than one pitch from that day on. At the onset, it is hard to tell what a situation will lead to in the future. Those that look unassuming may end up landing you a six-figure deal. Better prepare for all of them as if they were the chance of a lifetime.

Business Lesson

Never go into investor meetings with just one idea, always have several backup projects ready. It is often those plans that you have thought about the least that strike a chord with investors.

Be Persistent

Regardless of the blowback from the investors, I still pursued the music house idea. Once I had narrowed down the list of suitable talent, I started meeting them face to face to find out if we could work together. With about three composers I was in regular contact, and I began working with them on smaller projects to test the waters.

One guy in the group stood out, even though others were stronger composer. At least once a week, he would call and ask for new projects. He would regularly drop by the studio with new cues he had composed. It seemed he had little other work at the time, and he was hell-bent on changing that. I had planned to ask other composers for some jobs but ended up working with him most of the time, just because he was constantly present. Other composers were either too busy or lacked the courage to call all the time, so he came out on top through sheer persistence.

Years later, this composer landed an Oscar nomination for a short film he scored. He then went on to compose for a three-hundred-million dollar blockbusters movie, which boosted his career massively. It is clear to me how that happened. His persistence positioned him in the front of everyone's mind.

Business Lesson

When you want something, be persistent. Pursue your mission relentlessly. As long as you are polite, you can get away with it without annoying others. They will tell you when you crossed the line.

Stay Away from Wannabes

There is one stereotype you will often meet in Hollywood: The wannabe. This person has been living in town for several years (sometimes decades), and has tried and failed many times. Despite all hardship, he is still hopeful and "wants to be" successful. Strangely, project after project suffers the same fate. When you take a step back and ponder the actions of the wannabe, the reason becomes clear quickly. He has a weak support structure consisting of other wannabes, who all like to talk but do nothing to upgrade their knowledge and experience so they can actually compete. They are stuck in a loop of underachievement. Even if they came up with a good idea, it had nowhere to go. The people in their network would sabotage it consciously or subconsciously.

The wannabe has made failure a habit without admitting it. You will hear him complain about how the system is unfair to "artists." How someone else stole his ideas is also a favorite topic. Another one is how he abhors being commercial, and would rather "pursue real art than sell out." Consequently, he sets his sights on half-baked projects that are surefire disappointments from the onset. Some wannabes are masters in making others believe they are just on the brink of a breakthrough. Just talking about success is enough for them. This is an integral part of their underdog identity. They cling to it like chewing gum to a shoe sole. It may be amusing to listen to them for a while, but they are poison for anyone seriously trying to make his mark. When people tell you about how this time, they will for sure succeed, they may be of the wannabe sort.

Granted, you need to start somewhere. But when you have arrived in a big pool where you need to compete with talent from all over the world, you better have a track record and a strong motivation. Otherwise work with people who do. At the same time, always upgrade your craft and talents. As long as you mingle with those who have gotten used to hanging out on the ground level, you make it harder for yourself than necessary. Keep their excuses for their mediocrity out of your vocabulary. Better yet, avoid this group altogether. There are plenty of other interesting individuals available for you to meet and make friends with.

Business Lesson

Some people enjoy the part of the underdog. They keep themselves trapped in a perpetual loop of underachievement and self-sabotage. Stay away from them if you are serious about success.

Be Flexible

As soon as I had set up the basic infrastructure of my recording studio, my first order of business was to create a so-called "show reel." This would be a CD with samples of my music cues that would show my skills and ideas. I spent a few weeks to create about twenty short music clips that could find use in feature films. They ranged from comedy music clips all the way to sweeping action movie scores. With this CD and some printed material in hand, I attended film festivals where I would ambush directors with my pitch. I gave about one hundred such show reels away, with only modest feedback. Obviously, there were others trying to break into the film business as well.

Then, a miracle happened. Out of the blue I got a phone call from a young director who was looking for a composer. The only problem was that his movie was a horror film, the one genre I had forgotten to prepare music cues for. Whether I had experience in scoring zombie movies, the director asked. "Of course," I answered. "I am a huge horror fan." In a hurry, I would then write a few cues that I would send over to the director this same evening. This was my first job in Hollywood.

Just taking on a job without a clue how to actually do it is common in Hollywood. Everybody seems to be able to do anything. The attitude of being open and trying something that is out of one's comfort zone is refreshing. At the same time, it is also a risk, and people often bite off more than they can chew. At some point, I had a received a budget from a record label to make a music video. The selection of directors had come down to three who submitted a script and storyboard for the video. Some of them included pyrotechnics, intricate computer animation, and complex choreography – all for less than twenty thousand dollars. This is pocket change in Hollywood, and there was no way these directors could ever deliver. However, stretching their boundaries was normal to them. By being realists they would never get work. Promising things out of your league is how Hollywood does things. Whether the result is what the client imagined, is often secondary.

Business Lesson

When clients ask you if you are an expert in something, answer "Yes, of course!" Unless it is totally out of your league, you can always wing it later.

CHAPTER 2: NETWORKING AND COMMUNICATION

Networking is extremely important in Hollywood. Every day, there are events to meet people, strike new alliances, and forge new business deals. You should know how to handle these situations to make them work in your favor. Especially when you are starting out, these networking events will be valuable. Later, when you already have a network, you can skip most of them, as your relationships will sustain themselves. People are generally open to share, so if you have some friends in your circle who often attend these events, they may inform you regularly when they met someone who you should contact for business.

We will look beyond learning how to engage in small talk in this chapter. Other books cover this topic in great detail. Let's focus instead on the mindsets and perceptions that matter when you communicate with strangers. How you approach them is more important than the words you use.

Have a Good Lawyer or Two

Newbies to Hollywood are said to need three things: An apartment, a car, and an agent. The apartment and the car are obvious, but instead of an agent, a good lawyer may be even more important. They can have a double function in your business: Checking legal documents and connecting you to their existing network. Most people never think about that last part. However, some of the best-connected people in every industry are lawyers and accountants. It can help a lot to team up with the right legal partners. You may need more than one legal professional to fulfill these functions for you.

As always, when you add another team member to your network, check their references first. Since you need more than just legal advice from your attorney, also ask about their connections. Inquire if they will introduce you to their clients or colleagues who may help you advance your projects. It will surprise you how receptive most lawyers are to this suggestion.

Business Lesson

All your service providers have the added function of advancing your network through their contacts. When you hire a new support partner, make sure they add more than their formal services alone.

Be On A Mission

When you have a clearly defined goal, you will radiate confidence. This is what will help you build a strong network, especially when you moved to a new city or country and need to build up social and professional relations from the ground up. Being on a mission means you follow a charted course in your projects and your life. With dogged persistence, you follow through, regardless of public opinion. In Hollywood, this means you have something to do all the time. Others may be sitting at home, waiting for the phone to ring, but you have better things to do. Be interesting so that others pursue you. Being on a mission is powerful and attractive.

This is important in everything outside of business as well. Which goals do you have for your life? They are probably bigger than reacting to the demands of other people, paying the bills, and trying to make ends meet. Think about the big picture. What motivates you to get up in the morning? What will you do if you have achieved fame and fortune? Why are you doing what you are doing?

Hollywood is a destination for dreamers. All those who move there have some aspirations about becoming famous, wealthy, or making their mark in other ways. They often have a vague idea where they want to go, but a strong mission with a detailed game plan is lacking. You need to define this for you as early as possible. Write it down, and revise it when you see fit. This is personal, so there is no need to share this with everybody you meet, or – even worse – ask what they think about it. All those who have achieved success have been able to do so because their mission guided them. Adopt this mindset, and bond with others who follow the same trail.

Business Lesson

What is your mission in business and life? Know where you want to focus your energy and then do only that. Instead of reacting to external demands, live up to your full potential.

Looks and Perception Matter

Hollywood is a superficial place. Some go as far as calling it fake. It is the land of plastic surgery, with no body part spared. Even C-grade actors feel they need to get hair implants or other enhancements just to get a shot at the big time. Look at the famous actors on screen. Most of them had "work done," so it is easy to assume you should do so as well.

Looks matter, but in a different way from what most people believe. Sure, a news anchor needs to look young and fit, regardless of their age. Nobody likes to see a tired announcer on morning television. The same goes for a famous actor in a three-hundred-million dollar action movie. They need to the aura of being superhuman. After all, endorsement deals hinge upon the demographic that they appeal to. If an actress has less than "perfect" skin, how can she possibly endorse beauty products?

For everybody else, looks matter in a different way. More important than perfection is your confidence. This goes far beyond just physical looks. How many times have you heard that the car that you drive defines who you are? As long as your car is clean and undamaged, it is perfectly fine for most occasions. In all my time in Los Angeles, I was driving a family car, a Mercury minivan. Nobody ever judged me negatively because of it. And if they did, it was their loss. Conversely, I met people who drove leased German sports cars, in the hopes that they would help offset a lack of talent or determination. Some of them were so tapped out that they carried their entire net worth in their wallet. At the gas station, they had to calculate how many gallons they could afford to put in the tank so they still had enough cash to eat a meal that night.

Of course, if you live in a shoebox and drive a rusty clunker around town, you will send a strong message. Nevertheless, better stay away from the rabbit hole of chasing looks and perception. If you need to spend money to feel good, you have a problem. Unfortunately, much of Hollywood has that same problem. In the long run, chasing looks will distract you from gaining the confidence you need to succeed.

Business Lesson

Looks are important, but other things matter more. Make sure you present yourself in the best way possible, without chasing unhealthy or unrealistic ideals. You have more to offer than your nose and your car. If anyone tells you differently, it shows their own lack of confidence.

Stay Authentic

It is dangerously easy to assimilate behaviors, mannerisms, and speech patterns from others. My first Hollywood attorney advised me to pay attention to keeping my British accent intact (I had learned Oxford English in school). "We love people with British accents here, they sound so smart," she told me. However, neither the British accent nor any other accent was native to me, and I why should I put on an act? With time, the English accent faded and I soon blended in. It is always a little embarrassing when it transpires that someone is just putting on an act.

Language is a fertile ground for this, as it is so easy to adapt. The same goes for clothing styles and other accessories. When a white guy from Sweden dresses, walks, and speaks like Snoop Dogg, something seems slightly off. If you are always acting, people will sense this. They will never fully feel at ease with you. The same goes for hopping on any trend that comes along. A friend of mine was a specialist in this. He moved to Los Angeles from New York, where he had worked at an investment bank as a fund manager. Once in California, he quickly assimilated the lifestyle. He was now a vegetarian who practiced yoga for hours each day. A new girlfriend convinced him that he better become a fruitarian, so he did that. Then his money ran out and he took up work with a local investment firm. He went back to eating steak in a heartbeat. It had never felt quite genuine in the first place.

Because the whole town is putting on an act all the time, it takes an effort to keep the things you do and say authentic in Hollywood. When people move there, they are certain they will stay forever. But when they had enough and find themselves in a new place a few years later, their new style may haunt them. One such example are tattoos and other body modifications. Only in Hollywood will some of them be cool, for a while. Whatever you do to alter your image and your body, avoid procedures that are to your disadvantage later.

Business Lesson

Develop your own personality and refrain from copying others, even though that might seem cool at the moment. Instead of adopting slang, fashion styles, or mannerisms, impress with your ideas and projects.

Be Always On

One of my Hollywood music projects took an unexpected turn. Together with a singer from Japan, I had written some songs that went viral on Youtube. Over a hundred press articles in major music magazines followed, with invitations to play live shows in the United States, Europe, and Japan. All of this happened very quickly, just in the span of a few months. Both the singer and I were unprepared for this and blundered our way through the experience. Many lessons came out of this adventure. To this day, however, one of them stands out. I called it the "stuffed face."

One night, we opened for a famous band in a large concert venue in Hollywood. As always, there was a press reception with drinks and snacks before the concert. Some other musicians and the usual suspects from the major print magazines were there, but this time, a camera team from *E! True Hollywood Story* had joined them and interviewed celebrities backstage. Out of the blue, the reporter pointed towards the singer and me across the room. Was it possible that they wanted to film an interview with us? Seconds later the spotlight was in our face, but the timing was rather unfortunate. We both had just loaded up our plates at the buffet and were wolfing down burritos. The camera caught us red-handed. Clutching plastic plates and still chewing, our moths were so full that food would have fallen out if we attempted to answer the question of the journalist. Needless to say they quickly moved on to interview someone else. This chance never returned, and in all my time in Hollywood, I never was on TV. Taking a bite at the wrong time was to blame for it.

Business Lesson

When at a public event, be fully present. Instead of going there for the food, make sure you have a story to tell. If there is any press attention, take advantage of it.

Ask for Opinions

You have a written a film script and find yourself at a Hollywood networking event. By coincidence, you meet a studio executive who could potentially move your project forward. What do you say to that person? If you are like most people, you would kick off a monologue and pitch your idea. You explain it in much detail, unaware that you are talking yourself into a nervous frenzy. When you have finally run out of words and the other person is still there, you assume that it is now his or her turn to suggest improvements and extend an invitation for a formal meeting. In reality, if you have been hogging the conversation for any longer than thirty seconds, a decision maker will file a mental note that you are a nuisance. Pitching the wrong way seriously backfires.

There are better ways to get people interested in your projects. Better go for a two-way dialogue right from the beginning. Once you have given your elevator pitch of twenty seconds, get the other person to talk. Ask them questions, ask for their opinion. Ask if they have heard similar ideas recently. Find out if their studio would produce such a movie. By requesting their insight and opinion, you show your respect and treat them as an expert on the topic. Everyone likes being an expert.

The other person may have an interest in your idea. If they do, then chances are that you have presented yourself in a better light in a two-way conversation. If they have no interest, you have given them an elegant way to end the conversation right at the beginning. Without wasting their time you can always approach them when you meet them next time.

Business Lesson

When you meet someone important, avoid inundating them with details about your projects. Better ask for their opinion. It makes them feel important and gives you the opportunity to listen and learn something.

Check People's Motives

There are those who might have tried several Hollywood careers, but to little avail. Perhaps they arrived as hopeful actors, talented or less so, and did everything in their power to land a job. A short appearance as an extra in a TV series with a few words (if they are lucky) was all they have to show for it. When their money ran out, they took on a job as a waiter and started writing scripts. Instead of being actors themselves, at least they could imagine stories for them and tell them what to do. Competition is fierce, and scriptwriters a dime a dozen (just like actors, or musicians, or directors). When that has sunk in, many leave Los Angeles, somewhat disgruntled. Those who decide to stay in spite of their misfortune often take on jobs in film production. This is as close as they can get to the big screen. They start handling creative people, and are no longer one of them.

This may sound harsher than it is. Most people behind the camera made a deliberate choice to follow their line of work. Besides, there is also no shame in failure. I myself have made many mistakes that sunk projects, sometimes spectacularly. Regardless, I was never envious of those who had more success than me. When you detect that, be very careful. There will be characters in Hollywood who have a bone to pick with anyone who believes he or she can make it. They almost see it as their duty to knock them down in a passive-aggressive way. None of their advice is honest, it is all distorted with their own negative experience.

When I arrived in Hollywood, I was rather undiscerning and asked everyone I met for advice. Most people obliged, but the quality of their advice varied. "So you try to make it big, eh. Just like everybody else. Let's see how long you last." That's how one person opened the meeting. Needless to say that nothing useful came out of it. Another would tell me that formalities related to work permits would take "weeks, sometimes months." I later took care of all of them in one afternoon.

Beware of those who try to impose their own mediocrity on you. Use common sense. If someone is a has-been or was unsuccessful in the first place, why listen to their advice? There are plenty of open-minded, successful individuals around who are eager to help and encourage you.

Business Lesson

Some people are jealous of your efforts to seek success. They may inject insecurity into your plans. Stay away from them and free up time to meet those who help you and support your goals.

Assume Everyone is Important

When started my first music company in Los Angeles, I needed to set up a business support infrastructure. Part of this were insurance policies for myself and my business. I asked around with some friends and found an agent who seemed trustworthy. Other things besides insurance are easier to be passionate about, so I was anxious to check that box and move on to more important things. If possible, I hoped to get done with everything in one short meeting.

On the faithful day, the agent arrived at my house with crutches and an assistant carrying his briefcase. He had just undergone foot surgery, he apologized. A long scar on his foot, which he happily presented, confirmed that. A long story about how the injury followed. Then some banter about music and music production, pop music, film music, and his favorite composers. I mentally prepared myself to add one more hour to this meeting. It took me by surprise how much this man knew about pop music, given the fact that his hair was gray and he hardly seemed the type who would go club hopping. In detail he wanted to know about my studio, how I got started, what I was working on, my plans, and so on. As politely as possible I answered his questions. We even listened to some songs of mine. After he knew everything about my work, wrapping up the insurance took ten minutes. At least that was over now.

A few days later I got a phone call from the insurance man. He wondered if I had an interest in producing a song for his fiancée, who happened to be an accomplished singer/songwriter. No word of this had come across his lips at the our meeting a few days ago. It turned out he was just testing the waters if I was a candidate for future collaborations. I soon started work with the singer. The first song we recorded went so well that I ended up producing an entire album with her. Some of the songs even won awards. And all of this started at a meeting for business insurance.

Business Lesson

You never know who you are talking to and who in their network could help you advance your career. Always be polite and positive, even to strangers. He or she could be the one deciding about hiring you for a project.

Avoid Acting Like A Fan

After a few years in Hollywood, invariably you will get to know some celebrities. They may be singers, actors, or movie producers, who seem to lead a different life from the average person. However, once you know them personally, you realize that after all, they are just people like everybody else. Strangers who want to take their picture while they are waiting at the dentist can become annoying after a while. Most celebrities use an assistant to do their daily chores, and they put on black shades and an air of inaccessibility in public. This is often misunderstood as arrogance. But somehow, even famous people make new friends. So how are they doing it?

Just put yourself in their shoes. What would you feel like if strangers fawned over you, confessing their admiration of all the work you ever did? Imagine you eat at a restaurant and someone lumbers toward you. "Oh my God, I love your work, especially your role in the movie X! I can't believe I'm meeting you! Can I take a picture?" Do you think this is going to be an interesting conversation? If this happens everywhere you go, it will take a lot of strength to keep smiling and posing for pictures with strangers. At the end of the day, when you make contact with a person, what does it matter if they are famous? Just treat everyone normally. If they find you interesting and feel they wish to get to know you better, then so be it. Reducing yourself to a fan and inflating them into a deity will only make the gap between you bigger.

I was going to a house party and brought along some musicians I was working with at the time. They were from the Canadian countryside and had flown down to Los Angeles to record their album. When they saw the splendid mansion in Beverly Hills, they were taken aback. So much that they started taking pictures with their phones. In the kitchen, the indoor pool, the bowling alley, the hosts walk-in closet, and so on. Like tourists they stumbled through that house. The host finally took me aside and asked me to tell them to stop. Needless to say that these guys had used up all their credit with their amateurish behavior.

Being star-struck is a reflex that you should quickly overcome. Instead of admiring other people as a fan, better be interesting and unique yourself. This makes for better conversation, both for you and anyone you meet.

Business Lesson

Avoid behaving like a fan. When you meet someone famous or fabulously wealthy, refrain from fawning over them and from complimenting on their work. Better be interesting yourself and have something to say.

Avoid Gossip and Namedropping

Hollywood seems to need gossip like oxygen. A thriving industry has developed from this addiction, including more or less official celebrity blogs, celebrity magazines, and even TV channels. Paparazzi make a great living in town. Some of them have their own agencies and photo distribution networks. It is common to hear "insiders" tell you the latest secret about so and so, which you often have to promise to keep to yourself. A publicist I know boasted a tale about an A-list Hollywood actor who had allegedly courted several female stars to enter in a faux relationship with him (for public appearances and press purposes). One of them supposedly had told her stylist, who then told her friend, who then told someone on a set, where this publicist heard the rumor in passing. I doubt any of it had merit. Does this remind you of high school?

When I hear somebody gossip, I lose a little respect for them. Does this person have nothing else going on than telling half-truths about others? Mind you, these stories are never uplifting. They are always about some alleged blunder, some character flaw, or a misfortune. So why do people bother to recount them? Many in Hollywood seem to believe by uttering the names of celebrities, they command some of the limelight for themselves. As if there existed some secret bond with that person.

However, those who gossip are never the seriously connected people. They keep the private lives of their friends private, otherwise they would be kicked out of the inner circle quickly.

An acquaintance of mine was a specialist in gossip and namedropping. Most of her conversation consisted of stories about others, with a preference for semi-celebrities. She would go on about how some pop star did this and that; she knew, because a friend had reportedly been the star's assistant. Some famous rapper did who knows what. She also knew, because she had been at his house party. This person seemed to know everyone in town, and spent much time recounting anecdotes about them. I found them amusing at the beginning. Because she told them with authority, they seemed like facts. Needless to say that most turned out to be hot air. Once I started questioning her tales, it became clear she had nothing to back them up.

Business Lesson

Refrain from telling or spreading gossip. Successful people care about other things than the alleged misfortune of others. When somebody drops names of famous friends, be careful. Those with real connections rarely brag about them.

Indirectly Brag by Asking Questions

"If you don't toot your own horn, there will be no music," says author Allan Weiss. As always, there is a fine line between annoying people with your bragging and letting them know about your abilities so they can benefit from them. You need to know how to toot your own horn when you want to build or expand your network. You should let others know what you are capable of doing. Then they can either continue the discussion with you or introduce you to someone who could use your talents.

Hollywood is notorious for vane bragging and namedropping. At every party or networking event, you meet people who will go on endlessly about their heroic accomplishments and the celebrities that they are supposedly best friends with. Most of these tales are pure fantasy, or they happened way in the past. Those with something going on in their life right now have other things on their mind than what they did ten years ago or gossip about somebody else. There are better ways to present yourself in a good light.

Instead of making your own greatness the center of the conversation, it is better to convey subtle hints that make you look good in the eyes of others. As an alternative to telling them about your talents out of your own motivation, better get them to ask you questions. However, this requires that *you* ask some questions first. When they want to know more in return, interject in your answers what you want to say. This way, both participants in the conversation can tell each other what they are doing. Instead of simply giving one-liners as answers, they insert additional bits of information that show the scope of their abilities. Conversations of this kind have many reasons to progress. As a result, you may learn something unexpected or meet other people through introductions.

Some argue that such conversations are absolutely fake. Instead of honestly caring about what other people do, you just ask questions to lay the foundation for your hidden self-advertising. Sure, this is true. Regardless, it is how you toot your horn in Hollywood, even though it is somewhat insincere.

Business Lesson

You must brag a little about your accomplishments. Start conversations by asking questions about others. When they ask you in return, use your answers as vehicles for your self-advertising.

Be Brief

When you introduce yourself at a party or networking event, have your story together. As soon as you start rambling and going off on tangents, you will lose people's attention. I was having a meeting with a record company executive. The meeting took a long time, and it was mostly filled with the guy telling me how his record label was the best there was and how he could absolutely help my artists reach the next level in their careers. In the entire meeting, I got to speak perhaps one minute in total, at the most. This was a pity, as I had prepared an elaborate pitch about marketing plans, target audiences, and more, that I had hoped to present to him. In the short time I had to voice my thoughts, I hardly scratched the surface, but just responded to his questions.

My attorney later told me that it was common knowledge that executive "had the attention span of a gnat." Only pitches that were absolute dynamite had a chance of getting through to him. I had assumed that I would have his full attention. Instead of inflating my pitch with background information and data, I should have condensed it to a few sentences. Then I should have tested it with friends to see if it stuck. As often in Hollywood, this was the first and last meeting with this executive. I needed to make use of it right then and there.

Many people in Hollywood have a short attention span. When a decision maker opens the meeting with "talk to me," then you better fire your most important idea in as few words as possible. When you write them an email, anything longer than three sentences has a big chance of never being read. They will lose interest after thirty seconds, so better use windows of opportunity while they are open.

Business Lesson

Cut out fluff when you pitch ideas, and start with the strongest selling point. Never assume you will get enough time to go into detail. Make your idea immediately interesting, otherwise people will move on quickly.

Swim Against the Mainstream

Author Earl Nightingale reminds us that "If you can't find a heroic, successful role model, just look at what everybody else is doing and don't do that." Nowhere else does this apply more than in Hollywood. Even though most people intuitively agree with the statement, they still do the opposite. When I freshly arrived in Los Angeles, my first agent always offered plenty of generic advice. Since everybody else also read this and that industry newsletter, I also had to do it. Of course, I would also have to work for free to get a foot in the door (I had kept it a secret that I commanded six figure fees in my previous company). And it would take about seven year on average to work myself up the ranks in the studio system to get any meaningful work.

This "everybody else" talk has always irritated me. My entire life I never did the same like anybody else I knew and was successful. Why should I change that now? The same is true for you. Whether you are starting a new venture or run an existing business, do what you believe is right. Stick to your guns even if it your ideas are totally out of the box. Generalities like "this is how we always did it" will get you to the same place like everybody else, which is mediocrity at best.

When you network in Hollywood, avoid trying to blend in with all the others. Only those who stick out their head will be noticed. Otherwise, you will naturally end up with a network of mainstream players who will all keep each other down. Better swim against the stream and connect with those who do so as well. You will influence each other to excel even more.

Business Lesson

Never do what "everybody else" is doing. When you feel something is right, then go for it. This attitude attracts those who think different. Your network will become a launch pad for fresh ideas.

Always Be Positive

You may be used to conversations about how bad this or that movie was, or how someone you both know did something terribly embarrassing. While it is customary to complain about the weather or the annoyances of one's work elsewhere, Hollywood prefers to hear only positive news. Life is already tough enough, so why listen to another downer? Consciously or subconsciously, people stay away from those with a negative attitude. "Did you meet so and so yesterday?" – "Yes, but it seems to me he's a negative person." That is the last thing you want others to say about you when you try to build your power network.

Better focus on how you saw someone do a good deed, or how you enjoyed this or that musical performance. Focusing on positive stories may sound trite, but it is a major issue in conversation that most people are unaware of. Once they shift their focus to the lighter things in life, your discussions will take a different turn.

Speaking with other human beings is about more than information exchange. The main point is how we make each other feel. Do you enjoy feeling sad by the tragedy someone just told you? When you center on the bright side of life when talking with others, everybody wins. This is true in Hollywood and anywhere else.

Business Lesson

When you speak about positive events, you present a much better picture of yourself. Besides information exchange, communication is about how we make each other feel. Keep things light and bright and avoid negative stories.

Fake It Till You Make It – In a Good Way

When you are starting out in business, there is no way you have already amassed bragging rights to heroic feats. Hollywood suggests to "fake it till you make it," which means padding your story so it sounds like you already accomplished something important. It also means you need to drive an expensive car before you can afford it, so it looks like you are already a hotshot. We discussed cars already. When I moved there, the "standard advice" (notice the danger) was that if someone asks you what you do, you should answer that you have "several projects in various stages of completion." To me, this sounded like a line right out of a bad movie. Nevertheless, more than once, I heard this from people at parties, and it always sounded silly. This line always sounded to me like the other person was doing nothing all day but eat and watch TV. Hardly an impression you want to give at a networking event. There are far better ways to convey that you are working on exciting projects, even if you have yet to land your first deal.

Most importantly, you should know your mission by now. If this is the case, you will naturally take proactive steps toward your goals and self-start projects that will get you there. If you just moved to Hollywood, let's say as a screen writer, you should be writing all the time. Once you have a body of work, you would then pitch your scripts to directors. If someone at an event asked you what you are working on, you would obviously tell them about your scripts and what they are about. You can also say that you pitched them to so and so and that you hope they take them on as projects. Be excited about your mission. Why should you have to hide that you are still a startup? As long as you work on your mission and have something to show for it, what exactly do you have to fake? "Faking it," in this case, just means that you are will yet to become profitable, and this is no shame to admit.

Business Lesson

It is perfectly fine to start from zero. As long as your mission is clear and you follow it persistently, what do you need to fake? Speak about what you do at the moment instead of trying to project something that has yet to happen.

How to Deal With Annoying Pitches – Gracefully

When you are a guest at house parties in Hollywood, it is interesting to watch how celebrities and other VIPs deal with their admirers and fans. Naturally, there will be aspiring actors, singers, writers, and directors who approach them. Sometimes, they will just start a harmless conversation. More often, they will try to solicit their own work for consideration. Many people pitch their work in inappropriate situations. The easiest reaction is to tell them to get lost. This is how you handle them in a graceful way.

One evening, I was at a party together with a semi-famous record executive. Shortly after his arrival, there was a queue of eager singers forming who wanted to meet him. Plastic cup in hand, he was standing in the kitchen and fielded the impromptu casting call. If course it was annoying, but there is always the tiny chance of finding a diamond in the rough in the most unlikely places. One singer had sent him a demo tape and now wanted to know what he thought about it. "It was very good," he responded. I doubt he even remembered who she was. Another one offered up a rendition of a song that she had written. His comment: "That's very good." Did he tell these singer to leave him alone or call his office the next day? Did he offer his business card or critique the pitches? None of the above. Everything was just "very good." They all gave him CDs with their songs and contact information, hoping he would listen to them the next day. I became a witness of the disposal of these materials as well. They all went straight to the trash can.

You should never pitch your business in social occasions, unless people expressly ask you to. After all, people want to have fun, and they do hardly feel like listening to your business proposals. If you foist materials on them, know that they will end up in the garbage. Is this what you want when you spend time and money putting together your proposals? On the other hand, if you receive pitches at unseemly times, be polite. You can always deflect attention with a positive comment. Refrain from offering criticism or engage in discussions, unless you really want to.

Business Lesson

Avoid pitching at social gatherings. When you meet someone important socially, keep business matters out of the conversation. If others pitch you, be polite, but refrain from engaging in conversations or setting up meetings

Everybody Is a Stepping Stone

Making connections in Hollywood follows a different pattern than in other towns. You will have to prove yourself at all times, just as you should evaluate others regularly if they still bring value to your network. When you determine someone fails to pull his own weight, then it is time to let him go. If you find yourself slacking, then you will notice how others withdraw from you. Hollywood is a tough place, and anything but a welfare state. When you compete with the best of the best, you simply cannot afford to let others weigh you down or drain your energy.

A friend of mine told me about this early on. In fact, she complained about how everybody just saw other people as stepping stones. As long as they could get them somewhere, they became quickly best friends. Otherwise, no connection would ever be possible. The result was that relationships, both business and personal, had this strong opportunistic component. When everyone operates under the assumption that life is short and time is money, they have no other choice. They better take advantage of whatever circumstances they can while their window of opportunity is open.

Realizing the true nature of your Hollywood friendships may disappoint you sooner or later. Unless you understand how those trying to make it in this town function, it will be confusing. Just know that your network will never be static. As long as you can add value to the goals of others, you will be fine.

Business Lesson

Be aware of the fluid nature of your network: It should be win-win, helping you reach your goals. Unless everybody contributes, upgrade your contacts and be more selective.

All Roads Lead to Rome

There are different ways to become successful in Hollywood. Every success story is unique, and many of them had more to do with being at the right place at the right time than strategy. How you do something is more important than what exactly you do. Nevertheless, I had friends who insisted they knew the one and only recipe for Hollywood success. "Get a full-time job and try to launch a career on the side," was one of them. "Do anything to get in the door and then build up slowly," was another one.

"Forget about writing a hit. Write hundreds of songs and license them for multiple revenue streams." The list goes on. None of these ideas are wrong per se. They are just different from what I believed was right. When I objected, they would start becoming defensive, and I often had to deflate the situation to avoid a heated argument.

All of this is unnecessary. Why argue? Better just do it and let your actions and their results speak. At the end of the day it is irrelevant what exactly you did to make it work. As long as you get positive results, that is good enough. When new ideas come along, you may change course along the way. But when others need to persuade you that your approach is wrong and theirs right, better save yourself the argument. Let them inspire you with ideas, but do what you hold as true.

Business Lesson

Accept that others may have a different strategy for their business. Likewise, let others inspire you with ideas, but keep doing what you believe is true.

CHAPTER 3: BUSINESS MEETINGS

Meetings are in a league of their own in Hollywood. It can be surprisingly easy to get a first meeting because people in the entertainment industry are always on the lookout for talent. The tough part is the second meeting. Better think ahead when you walk into somebody's office for the first time. This chapter covers a few basics about Hollywood meetings you can use as a checklist.

Anything is Possible

In Hollywood, anything is possible. The city seems to have an accelerator that can work to your advantage in unexpected ways. When you have something that others desire and you are at the right place at the right time, you could find yourself in illustrious circles in the blink of an eye. You may be invited to very exclusive events where stars from the big screen now want to meet you. As a songwriter, you could be working with the famous singer you always admired when that accelerator kicks in. Last week you were still a barista at Starbucks wondering how to make ends meet, now you are sitting next to her in a Beverly Hills mansion, working on a song for the new album. Such is the promise of Hollywood. These is always a tiny chance the impossible might happen, so better recognize it when its time has come

One Sunday morning, I received an email from an employee at one of the largest record companies in town. He thought one of my tracks had potential, and wanted to listen to more songs of mine to see if there was something we could do together. I had had several such inquiries before, and they usually led nowhere. A few hours later, the same guy sent me another message, this time to one of my social networking profiles. Without expecting much, I arranged a meeting a few days later. While I was still walking in the street to the entrance, I could hear my song blasting from one of the offices. They seemed to have a party up there.

I expected a short conversation with the person who had sent me that email. Was I surprised when I was escorted to the penthouse office of the president of the label who had recently made the Forbes list of the world's most powerful people. Together with his team, we listened to my music for one hour. When I asked him what he had in mind, he said: "This track would be perfect for [insert huge megastar here]. I want [insert huge mega producer here] to work on it with you." I was speechless. Was this even possible? It seemed it was. Even tough my excitement was enormous, the deal fell through a few weeks later. This can happen. But I had seen what could have been possible. It worked out for a songwriter I knew. When he was visiting Los Angeles, he would crash on people's couches. Three years later, he was working with just about all the big stars in the world and moved into a twenty-million-dollar mansion in the Hollywood Hills. When things take off, they go fast in Hollywood. Even though the odds are against you, anything is possible.

Business Lesson

It may seem unrealistic, but there is always a chance for the unexpected. When the stars align for you, grab the chance and hang on. You may achieve your wildest dreams of fame and fortune much faster than you think.

Be Punctual

You may be used to arriving fashionably late and blaming the traffic for it. Or the phone call you absolutely had to finish. Or the dog that ran away. They may be polite about it, but nobody really cares about these excuses in Hollywood. If you are late, this reflects badly on you. It is always your fault. No one will tell you that, of course. They may just pulling the classic "I will absolutely call you next week to set up a meeting," which ends up in a loop that goes nowhere. If you are serious about starting a business, then avoid being late.

This was news to me when I came to Los Angeles. Believing that everything would be easy-going over there, I cared about anything but time management. When I was meeting someone in an area I was unfamiliar with, I trusted that I would somehow find my way and be there just in the nick of time. Being late up to fifteen minutes was perfectly acceptable in my hometown. Then someone told me that he always double-checked the route to an important meeting by driving there the day before. Just to make sure there were no unexpected construction sites or other blockages. He would find the building, familiarize himself with the parking structure, and study the floor plan so he knew exactly where the office was in which the meeting was to take place. He would sometimes be an hour early for meetings, and eat breakfast in his car. This makes little sense until you realize that in Hollywood, one single meeting could be a life-changing event. Since you only get one chance, you have to be on your best behavior. Otherwise you might blow it. Many people believe that those who cannot be punctual cannot be trusted in other ways either.

Productive people value their time above all else. One of my neighbors was a retired rock star guitar player from an eighties band. He had toured the world in private jets and had lived the good life. Celebrities follow a tight schedule and must show up on time. They can only do this with iron discipline and serious planning. So whenever I met with this neighbor for a meal or coffee, he would suggest an uncommon time like 10:10 AM or 2:25 PM. It later occurred to me that this man was running on a schedule partitioned in slices of five and ten minutes. 10:10 AM meant 10:10 AM, not 10:15 AM. In those five minutes he could have done something else, and time is money. Do you think this person would give you another meeting if you let him wait for fifteen minutes? Most people are less extreme, but you get the point. If you set a time for a meeting, that's the time you should show up.

Business Lesson

Always be on time. Traffic jams and other acts of God are no excuse if you are running late. You should have left home earlier in the first place. Every meeting may be life-changing, so treat people with respect and arrive on time.

Allocate Your Time

Taking meetings in Hollywood is a bit like speed dating. Every minute counts. You only have so much time in a day to find those people who are most helpful to you to accomplish your mission. When someone turns out to be less interesting than you initially thought, cut the loss and move to the next one. This may sound insensitive and mechanical, but it is how most people act in Hollywood, consciously or subconsciously. Time is money, and you have to allocate it where it yields the highest return.

A rule of thumb is to reserve thirty minutes for the first meeting. Unless things go exceptionally well, make sure you bring the meeting to a close after about twenty-five minutes. You should be out of the door after half an hour. In that time, you will have plenty of opportunities to find out if someone can help you to realize your projects. Unless it looks like they can, propose staying in touch. If they do, then set the next meeting where you discuss the project specifics. This second meeting can last as long as it takes to discuss the project. If you are looking at a rough cut of a movie together, then it may take two hours. Since you already determined that this is time well spent, your focus is now on landing the project. If for any reason, things turn out to be different from what you originally thought, then bump down this contact in priority and start from the beginning.

Allocating your time helps you to evaluate if someone is just a talker. Those people often have all the time in the world and will ramble endlessly about their former glory and all the magnificent plans they have for the future. Unless you set a clear framework for these meeting, they will drag on for hours. On the same token, know that the clock is ticking when you are in the hot seat and pitch an idea to somebody who agreed to meet with you. Thirty minutes is about the maximum you can expect for a first meeting in Hollywood. Better bring your point across quick if you want to keep people interested.

Business Lesson

Spend your time well. First meetings should last thirty minutes tops. If you decide to take it to the next step, set another meeting to discuss project specifics. When it becomes clear that your time would bring a higher return elsewhere, cut the loss.

Lead Meetings

When you have something that other people want, things begin to look up for you in Hollywood. You will receive invitations to meetings to "see if we can do something together." I felt honored when I got phone calls requesting my presence. Under the impression all I had to do was show up on time, I went into those meetings to see what they would offer. They would often tell me how much they liked my music, how great their firm was, and how they could do a lot for me and my projects. They would ask me a few questions, and then say "Great meeting you. We'll be in touch soon." I stumbled out of these meetings thinking everything went well. "They were pitching to *me*," I would tell my friends. Little did I understand that this was standard protocol. Unless I had outstanding ideas that would warrant another meeting, chances were slim that I would ever hear from them again.

When you are in a meeting, take the lead. Prepare a short pitch, make sure you demonstrate your vision and the creative firepower to back it up, and then test the other party to see if they would be a good partner to help you move it forward. Avoid going into meetings hoping that other people will do the thinking for you. You can take better advantage of these unique situations. Movers and shakers in Hollywood have hundreds of such meetings a month. At the end of the week, they rarely remember that they met with you. Unless, of course, you impressed them with an idea so big that it subordinated anything else they saw that week. Only then will you move your project up in priority and to the next step. When you lead in meetings, you have a much better chance of making that happen.

Business Lesson

Everybody loves a leader. Present your vision in meetings with as much impact as possible. Do the thinking yourself. Lead meetings, instead of expecting others to propose interesting projects for you.

Test Limits and Limitations

Have you ever pushed someone's patience to see how they reacted? This is the favorite pastime of five-year-olds, you may say. In Hollywood, however, it is common. You will encounter little tests of character woven into negotiations, meetings, and social occasions. Why would anyone do that, you ask? For the simple reason to see what happens, of course. In times of stress, you learn what people are made of. If someone cannot control his emotions, then better find out quickly before it matters.

Such a test may be as simple as making an demand that stretches the boundaries. Instead of having a package delivered to someone, ask them to pick it up at your office. Another trick is doing the exact opposite of what someone requested. In a coffee meeting, you would ask the other person what they want, and then bring them something else. "You want black coffee, no milk, got it." – A minute later: "Here's your coffee with milk." Does this seem infantile to you? Of course, but hey, we are in Hollywood.

It can be interesting to watch what people do in certain orchestrated situations. Let's say so have a coffee meeting with someone. When you both stand in the queue, ask to get a coffee for you while you go wash your hands and give him five dollars. Then see if he returns the change to you. Or assume you walk up to your car to drive somewhere with another person. After you have opened the passenger door for her with your key, see if she reaches over to unlock the door for you while you walk around the car to get in yourself. Or when you invite someone for lunch, see if they return the favor the next time around.

All this sounds silly, but be prepared to encounter these situations more often than you think. The way you handle them tells something about you, and you will draw some conclusions from the reactions of others. Sometimes you can push a bit to get more information. This may help you understand what doing business with them will be like later down the road.

Business Lesson

When you do business with someone, see how they react in certain orchestrated situations. Observe if they only think about themselves, or if they look out for you. This often foreshadows what will happen when the rubber hits the road.

Always Check References

Checking references is a no-brainer, but it is still often overlooked. Hollywood is the land of professional actors, so how can you know that somebody you meet is really who they say they are? Most people pad their resume with heroic feats that only took place in their head. Several times I met people claiming to be "producers" who had trouble backing this up with any real credits. Obviously, nobody else had ever asked them questions about their production experience.

Especially when you need to hire someone, you need to be able to trust them. Make sure they provide references and then call them all up. If none of them picks up the phone, something is wrong. Make it a habit to ask unexpected questions, for example, if people use drugs regularly. What will you do if you find out that someone is wanted by the police, right after you paid them the first installment of a contract? You may find this improbable, but anything is possible in Hollywood. To prevent discrimination in the hiring process, the law prevents you to ask interviewees how old they are. However, you should ask for some form of ID when you meet them. Many people use fake names, so feel free ask for their driver's license to double-check.

When you find out something is wrong, part ways immediately but amicably. Make a note to yourself to check references even more thoroughly the next time around. You cannot afford to waste time with a bad hire or a professional relationship that turned out to be the opposite of what it looked like.

Business Lesson

Hire slow and fire fast. Ask for and check references of people's work as well as their character. Call up former clients or employers. When you find out something is wrong, walk away from the deal immediately.

The Business Lunch

In Hollywood business lunches, the focus is more on *business* than on lunch. Most people blunder their way through lunches without even noticing it, and they often lose previously gained respect as a result of their behavior. Come on, I hear you say, how difficult can it be to have lunch? When you notice that they often double as character tests, you better up your game. You thought you already made it and the lunch is a mere act of kindness, but in reality it is the ultimate test that will make or break the deal.

First of all, make sure you get to the place of the meeting early. Become familiar with the café or restaurant and then wait for the other party to arrive. Avoid going to the meeting starving. Make sure you ate a good breakfast and perhaps a little snack just before the lunch so you can concentrate on doing business. Wolfing down your lunch hardly makes a good impression. In general, let the other party order first and then order something similar. If it turns out the other person is a vegetarian, better refrain from ordering a bloody steak. Best is a small soup dish or salad. Order a small plate so you have more time to address the issues you would like to address. Make sure your lunch is a mere subplot in the business part of the meeting.

You need to have your business agenda planned in your head when you go to the lunch. Leave all paper at home, such as prints of your latest script, unless the other person expressly asked you to bring them. Remember, you want to move each interaction to the next one. If the other party likes what you have to offer, then set up the next meeting to discuss a project in more detail. The business lunch is a good opportunity to suss out the other party informally, and to see how they tick. When you find common ground, suggest the next steps. What those are should be clear before the meeting.

When it is time to pay the bill, it is perfectly normal to split it. When you meet a high-powered executive, he will most likely invite you. Never expect that, though. An air of entitlement rarely goes over well. When you are invited, offer that you pay your share. No need to invite others because they took the time to speak with you. Just calculate in your head what you owe, add fifteen percent for the tip, and put the money on the table.

Business Lesson

In business lunches, the focus is on business. Think of them as character tests or informal meetings that allow you to set the stage for later formal meetings. Suggest what you see as the next steps at the end of the lunch and take it from there.

Insist on Your Beverage of Choice

An attorney taught me an excellent Hollywood business lesson when we went to a meeting with a studio to talk about a contract for a project. It is common to offer people something to drink beyond coffee or water at meetings. Most people are on a diet anyway, or are afraid of staining their whitened teeth with black coffee. Offices therefore have a well-stocked refrigerator with a variety of non-alcoholic beverages. When the assistant asked my attorney what he wished to drink, he requested a Diet Coke. "Uhm, we don't have that. But we have Diet Pepsi. Would that be OK?" – "No thanks," replied the attorney. "I will have nothing then." – "Bottled water, perhaps?" the assistant tried again. "No, I wanted a Diet Coke." Somewhat flustered, the assistant shuffled off. I later asked the attorney why he was so insistent. His answer blew me away: "This was a test. If they can't come up with the drink I want, they need to prove harder that they can offer me something good in the deal." In his mind, they would have to make the disappointment with more favorable deal terms. Things are obviously a little more complicated than that. But in the next meeting at that studio, there were several cans of Diet Coke placed right there in the middle of the table.

Food and drink are a big deal when you work on projects in Hollywood. People often judge companies by their catering on set. Even though every film shoot has catering, the quality varies widely. Some offer slices of Pizza, while others serve sliders and vegan chocolate cake. When your status in Hollywood rises, film studios or concert producers may ask you for your favorite foods and beverages. You will then find them in your backstage room. To make an effort to accommodate VIPs is paramount in building long-term relationships.

Business Lesson

Test business partners for their willingness to accommodate you. Small signs like serving your favorite beverage set a positive tone for future projects. Pay attention to the food and beverage preferences of your business partners as well.

CHAPTER 4: DEAL-MAKING

Network building, meeting potential business partners, and pitching projects are all good and well. But the only thing that counts at the end of the day is making deals. Unless you can advance your efforts to this crucial stage, your business will have difficulty taking off. Unfortunately, it is easy to get caught in a loop of endless pitching and network building. This is like a startup remaining in stage one, without ever making a return on investment. In this chapter, we examine a few steps that can help you to jumpstart deal-making mode.

Turn Down Free Work

Those who are new to a city often believe they have yet to earn their keep by working for free or for very little money. This the case in every big city and industry outside of Hollywood as well. Free interns are a staple in every larger corporation, especially in creative industries. Starting at the bottom may work for someone with zero experience fresh out of college. But if you have ideas for a business or new project, it will rarely get you to your goal fast enough. But I need to get in the door first as a free intern, I hear you say. Wrong. If you feel that the only way to do build business relationships is by lowering your value, please revise your attitude. You must come from a position of strength right at the beginning. Once you are the person who works for free, it will be difficult to shake that stigma.

The only time working for free makes sense is when you believe you bring zero value to a commercial enterprise. In this case, you would learn from those doing the paid jobs, asking them questions, without contributing anything productive. The reality looks always different, of course. Non-paid labor works hardest on menial jobs, like making coffee or cleaning up tables littered with pizza boxes from the meeting. If you bring value to someone else's project, why should you give that away for free? People will readily exploit your talents and your time if you allow them. If they work on commercially viable projects, then they have a budget to accommodate anyone who can make that project better. Demand that for-profit enterprises pay you for your work. If they refuse, then you may need to upgrade your skill set first so you contribute value to others. There are better ways to be doing that than running errands and bringing people coffee. Especially when all others around you are drawing a salary.

Another case of free labor is widespread in Hollywood: The amateur project. A writer/director friend of mine wished to land a deal with a film studio for a feature film. He intended to produce a short trailer for his movie as part of his pitch presentation. Since he had no budget to produce this trailer, he asked me if I could write and produce the music for it. Once he had raised the funding for the project, I would be on board as the music composer. This sounded good enough for me at the time, and I spent weeks in my studio on the music. Of course, the project went nowhere and the movie ended up never being made. Such is the fate of nearly all amateur projects.

It is nice help your friends, but working for free regularly is a bad business decision. When you do, avoid confusing this with working on your business. Good things may come out of it, but that is a long shot. Running a successful business has little to do with playing the lottery, in Hollywood and anywhere else.

Business Lesson

Never work for free or cheap just to get your foot in the door. If you think you need additional skills, then train in other ways before you offer your services.

Assume Failure

When it comes to negotiating deal terms, many successful people in Hollywood assume failure with their projects. They will of course express that differently. It is mainly their actions that speak volumes. They prefer collecting as much money upfront, and as little as possible on the backend. Sure, Tom Cruise may have a deal for some points in the success of one of his franchises. Those are almost certain to become blockbusters. We are talking about something else here. Anything that is far from a sure bet falls under this category. Endorsement deals, for example. When a brand wants to secure a star as the spokesperson for their advertising, they will most likely demand huge fees upfront. Whenever a celebrity enters unknown territory, they implicitly assume that the venture will tank.

Most upstarts in Hollywood do it the other way around. They work for free, sometimes for several years, on the promise that if a project takes off, they will take part in the upside. Unfortunately, this almost never happens. If they modeled their approach after those who are successful, they would see that they must leave the free zone as soon as possible. Unless they are getting paid for their work, they will never make it. Assuming failure of all the projects they work on can help them make better decisions. They turn them down to begin with or will opt in the favor of payment upfront than on the backend.

How much money they are going to pay for your services is also a test of your counterparties. When they have no cash, perhaps because they have a "liquidity problem," then think for yourself if you should do business with them. Do you believe that they will manage their finances better with this particular project? Better seek out people who are already successful. Should their project fail, at least you got your money upfront.

Business Lesson

Prosperous people demand as much payment as possible upfront. If there is no cash, then the project is most likely unprofessional and will probably fail. Stay away from commissions. They rarely end up being profitable.

Beware of the Middlemen

Hollywood is well-known for all kinds of deals that turn out to be to the disadvantage of artists. It is the land of the five-percenters, the ten-percenters, and the twenty-percenters. These are professional gatekeepers such as attorneys, agents, talent managers, or business managers who demand a percentage of your earnings in exchange for their services. It is common for agents and talent managers to earn money this way. After all, they worked hard to land work for you. If they receive a bigger incentive, they may hustle even more and make you famous faster, or so the reasoning goes.

Attorneys and even accountants charge commissions, usually in the range of five percent. Ask yourself if it makes sense to pay an accountant fifty thousand dollars if you earn a million in a year. After all, their work is still the same since the time you only earned ten thousand dollars. The same holds true for managers who demand to receive a commission on any work you do, besides the projects they landed for you. Suppose you make a deal on your own, is it then fair to have to pay twenty percent of the fee to a manager who had nothing to do with it?

Limit commissions to the work that third parties directly bring in for you. It is always better in the long run to pay anyone with a flat fee or hourly. If they refuse, then ask yourself if you feel comfortable with the arrangement. The excuse that "everybody here works like this" is seldom reason enough.

Business Lesson

Avoid indentured servitude. Pay people who work for you, but stay out of deals that exploit you. Instead of giving up a commission on your deals, pay a flat fee.

Make Demands and Push Back

Another Hollywood minefield is writing up contracts for your deals. In boilerplate, they lay out general terms, payment schedules, deliverables, and so forth. When I read the first drafts that my attorney wrote for me, I often wondered how anyone in their right mind would accept the terms that the contract demanded. They were all entirely in my favor. Out of fear that some of the clients would rather drop the project and find someone else to work with, I suggested putting more favorable terms in the contract to avoid losing the work. "No way," my attorney said, "we're all grown-ups here. If they don't push back and come up with a counteroffer, then it's their fault."

This was a big change from how I had conducted business in the past. Playing power games was new to me. I had always made sure that the other party got an equal benefit out of the deal. In Hollywood, however, you need to show strength. The other party can defend itself, so why should you pull any punches? Make sure the deal is right for you, and defend the terms vigorously. Nobody will give you anything unless you ask for it.

At the same time, also be aware that the contracts that others offer to you follow the same pattern. You need to push back as much as you can so they take you seriously. Instead of signing worldwide contracts, exclude certain rights and territories from the contract. Instead of agreeing to have someone use your intellectual property in perpetuity, limit the term to five years. Always push back and think about your own benefit. If Hollywood can do this, so can you.

Business Lesson

When you negotiate deal terms, start with exactly what you want. Avoid pulling any punches in your contracts. Offer concessions only when the other party makes you do it. Push back on anything they offer

What's In It For Them

The most powerful motivator in Hollywood is self-interest. When they see an advantage to themselves, people may green light projects far inferior to others without such benefits.

A friend of mine was a producer at a TV station. Like most others in Hollywood, he had also written several scripts that he hoped to shop to studios for production. On one such occasion, an executive who believed in my friend's abilities as a writer had taken his script under his wing and pushed it forward aggressively. When it came to the budget for the film, an unexpected hurdle came up. The executive insisted on bumping up the marketing cost by several hundred thousand dollars. My friend did budgeting all the time in his day job, and he was convinced his numbers were correct. He kept on trying to convince the studio executive that there was really no need for a higher marketing budget. The discussion went back and forth for a few weeks, until it finally stalled. The executive abandoned it and moved his attention on other projects. My friend said that only years later the situation became clear to him. The higher budget was for something else than marketing. It was meant to find its way into the bank account of the executive. When this incentive disappeared, he discontinued the project.

Nobody is suggesting you offer bribes to land your deals. But you should clearly point out the benefits that your business partners get from a deal. When projects stall, maybe the decision maker needs to see better what's in it for him.

Business Lesson

When you present projects and ideas to others, make sure you address their self interest. If they see that there is something in it for them, money or otherwise, they are more likely to help you.

Price is Unimportant When You Have What Others Want

When you have something that others want, you can demand almost any price in Hollywood. Why else would an actor receive twenty million dollars to star in a movie? It is supply and demand at its best. If talent is scarce, they demand large fees. When there is a lack of time and you can deliver, prices go up once more. You will see houses on the market in Beverly Hills selling for tens of millions. In this price range, a few million more will rarely break the deal. Especially when the buyer fell in love with one particular property and just has to have it.

On the other hand, if people have little need for what you have on offer, you will be on losing ground. Those with plenty of money rarely watch every dollar they spend, but they will often keep track of every cent. Who cares whether a house costs twenty or twenty-one million? But paying a house cleaner three dollars more per hour is a major deal. Better be the expensive house than the replaceable hired hand.

A friend had asked me to help her select an electric piano for her new home. With my experience from building my recording studio, we zeroed in on three particular models ranging somewhere between two and three thousand dollars. This is in the upper price range for keyboards, so we went to some large music stores in town, in the mood for haggling. However, being a singer who was used to the sound of real pianos, the electronic models fell short of meeting her expectations. One of the stores we went to also had a showroom with grand pianos. As soon as we started playing them, it became obvious that nothing beats the real thing. My friend finally settled on a grand piano for over forty thousand dollars. She could afford it. Meanwhile, the sales clerk was scratching his head. We entered the store as price-conscious customers, looking at the price tags of the cheaper models. All this went out the window in the piano showroom. Regular customers usually have a narrower price range. But in Hollywood, the sky is the limit.

Business Lesson

Always offer several price options to your clients. They may choose one that exceeds what they told you they wanted to spend originally. When people are desperate for what you have to sell, charge more.

Plan for the Worst, Including Death

When you get down into the nitty-gritty of contracts for business deals in Hollywood, you would be surprised at how little trust the legal profession puts in people's ability to deliver, stay true to their word, finish the product, or even to stay alive. On more than one occasion, contracts I saw included worst-case scenarios beyond what you would wish upon your worst enemy. From disability to death, no stone was left unturned. When millions of dollars are at stake, trust goes out the window. Just look at this short dialogue from the film *Tropic Thunder*.

Rick Peck (Matthew McConaughey): They're going to kill him!

Les Grossman (Tom Cruise): And we'll weep for him... in the press. Set up a scholarship in his name, and eventually - I'm talking way, way down the road - we file an insurance claim.

Studio Executive (Bill Hader): Preferably before the end of the fiscal year. Actually, the claim alone would net us more than the movie would lose. (Smiles.)

How many business contracts of yours include a death clause? How about getting seriously injured on the job? In general, there is little need to plan for every single contingency. Nevertheless, after working in Hollywood, I started taking worst-case scenarios into account. Seldom in written contracts, but in my mind. In the rare instances they happened, at least I was prepared.

Business Lesson

Why count on your luck and assume everything will run smoothly in your projects? Plan for scenarios and discuss them with your business partners. No need to assume a disaster, but know what to do if it happens.

CHAPTER 5: HOW TO MANAGE PROJECTS AND PEOPLE

Leadership is just as important in Hollywood as in Fortune 500 companies. Los Angeles has the reputation of being easy-going and relaxed, but show business is still a business like any other at the end of the day. You need to display CEO qualities if you want to make it in this town. We will explore how to do this with a Hollywood twist in this chapter.

Get Others To Work For Free

When I said you should avoid working for free, I was on your side. But when you are in a position to ask others to work for free for *you*, Hollywood is a goldmine. Will you find many individuals who believe they must earn their keep by starting at the bottom. Is it fair to exploit the self-consciousness of people to your own benefit? Regardless, it is what Hollywood does every day, all day.

Without free labor, most Hollywood projects would hardly get off the ground. Interns run errands like sending scripts via FedEx, file headshots, and join you in meetings so it looks like you have staff. They organize auditions, stock the catering table, and pick up guests in their own cars. Those working for free will seldom deliver high-quality work. Regardless, if you give them clear instructions, they can save you time and money.

Many accomplished film companies tried to get me to score demos for trailers and commercials for them for free. They always used the same arguments: "Nobody knows you in this town, so you have to get some *credits* under your belt first." Or "If you do this for us for free, we may *consider you in the future* for paid work." Or "This project will be pro bono, but it will give you *experience and exposure*." I would have none of it. But I learned which keywords they use to get others to work for free.

As long as you are transparent with your labor force about the work you expect them to do, they are free to accept or reject it. We are all adults here, so if they are fine with your terms, why should you feel sorry? If this sounds too callous, just sugarcoat it with a smile and treat them to a coffee from the vending machine. Now that is cold. Welcome to Hollywood.

Business Lesson

To save money, try to get others to work for you for free. Be upfront with them about the terms of payment, but point out that they gain experience and exposure.

You Are Much Stronger Than You Think

Have you ever been awake all night? Do you remember the next morning? Most people will probably feel a little sorry for themselves. The lack of sleep dominates their conversations during the day. After all, it is out of the ordinary that they sleep less than six or seven hours a night. If it happens, it derails the whole day.

When my companies started taking off in Hollywood, working all night was no exception. Sometimes I needed to finish a project due the next day and just had to bite the bullet. When the client meeting took place in the morning, I needed to present the work and look refreshed. Of course I was tired, but the quality of my sleep was the last thing that concerned anyone here. They had an interest in completing the project and earning money with it. I as the service provider had to deliver, end of story.

In this time, I learned that how we feel comes down to our attitude. I went with little sleep sleep for seventy-two hours on several occasions. After I learned that I could do it, the prospect of a night in the office had little power to faze me. I learned to take catnaps in my car, on concrete floors, or in coffee shops before the other person would arrive for a meeting. If I had five minutes available to catch up on sleep, I did it. Handling heavy machinery or driving on the freeway was out of the question, but I learned that my physical limits lay way beyond what I previously thought possible.

When I hear someone complain about how he got up a five o'clock in the morning and is now extremely tired, I have to shake my head (just in my mind, of course). Most people can do much more than be give themselves credit for.

Business Lesson

Your limits are far beyond of what you think is possible. Instead of complaining about inevitable situations, change your attitude about them and toughen up a little. How much more you can accomplish will take you by surprise.

Stay Out of Arguments With Clients About Technicalities

Despite how tough some people in Hollywood say they are, as soon as someone higher up the food chain demands something, watch them turn into mush. "Yes, of course, that's exactly what I was thinking as well," they may respond to a suggestion so wrong, that everyone in the room is biting their tongues. They will rarely carry out what the other person wanted. They just save themselves the argument at the moment, and then conveniently forget about the conversation.

When I had clients in my recording studio, it was very common for them to voice suggestions of their own. Mind you, it is incredibly difficult to talk about music. Even if you are a recording engineer or producer. Still, everybody has their opinion. Clients often thought that this or that instrument needed to be louder in a song. So I turned it up. Some thought that the bass was too weak. So I made it stronger. The singer sounded too harsh. I made the voice softer. You get the point. As soon as they went out the door, I listened to their suggestions. In some instances, they made the song better. I undid everything else and never brought up the subject again.

I also saw producers arguing with clients in their studio. When the client suggested something, they would roll their eyes and explain why this or that change made little sense. They lost hours doing this, and gave their client a negative vibe in the process. Arguments about technical matters are seldom necessary. Happily carry out clients' suggestions, Hollywood-style. Then conveniently forget about them after they walk out the door.

Business Lesson

When clients suggest a technical change in your work, better save yourself the argument. Just accommodate them for the time being and later undo what makes no sense.

Only Results Matter

Have you ever given someone a task to complete over the weekend? Has that person then shown up on Monday morning with some excuse why it was simply impossible to do it? This may be fine elsewhere, but in Hollywood, you get nothing for trying. A promise without a result is unacceptable. Yes, this is pedantic and seems at odds with the easy-going reputation of Los Angeles. But business is business, anywhere in the world. When egos fly high, some things are slightly exaggerated. People may get fired for making a promise they failed to keep, regardless of how insignificant the promise was. Since everyone is always on probation in Hollywood and you are only as good as your last job, professionals are extra keen on delivering.

After a few years in the business, I started demanding the same thing as well. When people said they would *try* to do something, this became a red flag immediately, and ultimately a filter to assess people's work. You have to show at least something for your efforts, however small that may be. Once you demand this from your employees, it is astonishing what they achieve. Good enough is often sufficient, especially under time constraints. Clients will rarely notice if you spent one hour or one week more on a project, as long as it fulfills certain basic requirements. A results-oriented mindset has saved me a lot of time and money since my Hollywood days.

Because Hollywood is only interested in results, anyone can perform a job, as long as they are doing it well and follow through. Companies are quick to outsource skills they lack in-house. This can work to your advantage if you are new in town. Demonstrate that you will deliver, and you may find work sooner than you think.

Business Lesson

Promote a results-oriented mindset. When employees get used to deliver something instead of coming up with excuses why they delivered nothing, their productivity will skyrocket.

Doing a Good Enough Job Will Keep You on the Team

You will inevitably meet people with a sustainable stream of high income in Hollywood. They may have a long-term engagement to act in a string of TV shows, are scoring feature films with a group of directors, or have other steady clients who enjoy working with them. I have often asked myself how such arrangements came about. Those actors, composers, and other creative individuals were very good at what they were doing, but others were better. This must have been a matter of something beyond the quality of their services alone. Why would a director refuse to try a new composer who might be better? Why would a recording studio always call on the same voiceover artist? And why would someone keep a personal assistant, even though she repeatedly made unnecessary mistakes? At the end of the day all of this comes down to two things: Personality and laziness.

The people in these positions are generally easy-going individuals and pleasant to be around. They are willing to try out things that the client suggests, even when it is out of their area of expertise. They will accept criticism without much complaint. So much about the basic traits of their personality. They also deliver a steady stream of good enough work that fulfills basic requirements. This is where laziness comes in. Why should the client change the team when everything works smoothly? Sure, the engine may run even better, but why take the risk? Someone I worked with paid eight thousand dollars a month to her house cleaner. She agreed this was too much but she shied away from taking a risk with new staff. At least everything was predictable with the current person, who felt irreplaceable and raised her rate to a ridiculous level. Giving the client no excuse to fire her was good enough to keep her in this cushy situation.

The same goes for creative work. As long as a composer consistently delivers acceptable work on time, a director will think twice before replacing him. A new person may be more talented but he could screw up the project when it matters. This risk keeps newcomers out of the project. They will only get a chance when it was an absolute necessity to fire an incumbent team member. And for that to happen, grave misconduct or a serious rift must have taken place. As long as team members keep projects on even keel, they will all stay on board for a long time.

Business Lesson

Be easy to work with and deliver predictable quality. Existing clients will often keep you on their team out of fear of taking a risk with somebody new. When you are in somebody's inner circle, work that is "good enough" suffices to keep you there for a long time.

It's All Sales and Marketing

When breaking new artists, the music industry often spends nine dollars to make ten. Ninety percent of the budget flows into advertising. Tiny margins drive a multi-billion-dollar industry. Without aggressive sales efforts, the entire entertainment industry would implode. Likewise, Hollywood is one big marketing machine. If it stopped bombard us with ads for new movies, television shows, pop songs, and computer games, how would we know they existed? The one with the loudest voice wins.

Advertising icon David Ogilvy wrote that "in the modern world of business, it is useless to be a creative, original thinker unless you can also sell what you create." Hard work and exceptional product rarely guarantee sales and success. You need to let people know what you are doing. I often focused too much on creating products according to the highest technical standards. When I came to Los Angeles, I noticed that this would hardly get me anywhere. Better have a great idea, make a good-enough product, and then hustle relentlessly. You may have asked yourself why this or that song could ever become a big hit. Relentless hustling, that's how. Sales and marketing trump exceptional talent any day.

Does this mean that you can sell just about anything if you spend enough on advertising? A horrible product will always flounder, regardless of its marketing budget. Hollywood box office flops such as *Gigli* and *Speedracer* earned just a small part of their cost. But as long as you produce something that is good enough and sell it aggressively to the right audience, then you are off to the races.

Business Lesson

Become familiar with sales and marketing, they are essential skills in any business. Marketing a good-enough product will yield greater success than building the perfect product that nobody knows about.

When Things Get Strange, Stay Cool

In Hollywood, anything goes. People may break into song in an investor meeting. They may suggest everybody hold hands do a Hawaiian chant. Someone may have overdone it with plastic surgery, and their implants or hairpiece look ridiculous. Someone may have an unfortunate name, such as Kuntz or Schmuckler. A person introduce himself to me as Fast Wind. "Hi, I'm Fast Wind. What's your name?" Some people in Hollywood spot odd accessories. Like my landlord, who owned hundreds of commercial real estate properties. Despite being over sixty-years old, he had shoulder-long bleached hair with neon-colored strains woven into it. His fingernails were each half a foot long (about twenty centimeters). They were painted with cat figures and flowers and were adorned with tiny diamonds. He was a wealthy businessman, but it was hard to keep a straight face when I negotiated the lease for my office with him.

Most encounters are less funny. While you are having an ordinary business meeting, a person might start sobbing uncontrollably. This has little to do with the deal you proposed, it is a movie running in their head that prompted this. Who knows what they have been through. Still, in a place where people's emotions are bubbling over at the slightest trigger, better prepare yourself for surreal experiences.

I could continue with many more such stories. The important thing to remember is to keep a straight face and stay cool. When a situation so grotesque happens that you want to blurt out the witty comment on the tip of your tongue, stop yourself. Also refrain from staring. Better be professional. Ignore it and act as if everything was perfectly normal. As long as people deliver what they promised, there is no problem. Follow your business agenda. If they follow up their strange behavior with erratic actions to your disadvantage, make a mental note that the other person may be a nutcase. On the same token, you can do almost anything you want in Hollywood, as long as you hold up your end of the bargain.

Business Lesson

In strange situations, refrain from making witty comments. Stay cool and act normal. As long as people keep their part of a business obligation, they can do (almost) anything they want.

Beware of Your Assumptions

Superficial attributes can lead to wild assumptions. If someone drives a fancy car, does this mean he is successful? On the other hand, a guy looking like a hippie may turn out to be a billionaire. As soon as you start to do the thinking for other people, you enter difficult territory. Better let them tell you in person what they can and will do. "But I assumed he/she would…" is a phrase that will often lead to headache and heartache. Better stay off this slippery slope for good.

In Hollywood, the same logic applies to business. Unless you specify your expectations for a project, it will rarely magically take place the way you like it. I had been invited to play a concert at a film festival. Together with the festival organizer, I started to put together the performance. It required renting expensive sound equipment, staff to build the stage, lights, and so on. Normally, when a musician plays a concert, he will show up, do his act for an hour, and then leave. The concert organizer pays him a flat fee. It slowly dawned on me that this guy expected it to be the other way around: I would organize and pay for all the technology of the live show, and on top of that perform for free. He stopped short of saying this openly. I may have assumed he would foot the bill, but did he say he would? As expected, when I brought up the subject, the whole thing fell apart.

Many people start projects on their assumptions. Too late they realize they are flawed, and it has become too difficult to extricate themselves from the situation. They feel their kindness has been taken advantage of, which is obviously true. At the same time, it is their fault. Others can only mislead you when you let them. You need to build up your confidence and make it a habit to speak up. Nowhere is this more important than in Hollywood.

Business Lesson

Do you assume that others will look out for your interest or do what you expect them to do? Instead, better check project details and leave nothing open to interpretation.

Think Only One Step Ahead

When I came to Hollywood, I originally wanted to write epic orchestral film scores. After putting together my show reel and pitching to directors, I realized many other composers were much stronger with classical film scores. I had to change my business model and focus more on my strength, electronic film scores and sound design. After working on some film scores with this style, people began to ask me to produce electronic pop music. This was beyond my original plans, but when the opportunity presented itself, this skill turned out to be in demand.

You will hear similar stories from most people in Hollywood. "I never thought I'd be a writer," a neighbor of mine said. He originally moved to the Los Angeles to work as a real estate agent, but when the economy tanked, he went back to college. His roommate went to an audition for a sitcom, so he joined him and got the part. On set, he met his future wife who convinced him to turn the short stories he wrote as a hobby into a movie script. You already know how the rest of the story goes.

To reach your vision, you should map out your strategy into milestones that you can meet one by one. Of course it is good to think one step ahead. However, a rigid plan to achieve your goals may blind you to new opportunities that come along. As long as you follow a trajectory but stay flexible to unexpected twists and turns, this is the best you can do in Hollywood. The biggest successes are often those that are on the periphery of what we initially aimed for.

Business Lesson

Have a strong vision but keep an open mind to unexpected events. It is often the unexpected that will end up being our greatest success.

Make Decisions, Even if They Are Wrong

Just as your employees should adopt a results-oriented mindset, you as their manager and leader also have to deliver. When a multimillion dollar movie is on hold because someone has trouble making up one's mind, the studio suffers serious losses. Just making a decision, any decision, often saves the day. Leadership is confidence. What you decide to do may stem from a thorough analysis or from your gut feeling, as long as you *do* decide.

I was recording a voice over for a commercial. From the beginning, the project was on rocky terrain, mainly because a committee had the task of deciding on the creative direction. It dragged on and on, until there were just a few days left before the deadline, with no decision made on which speaker to hire. The client was unsure about the kind of voice he wanted for the commercial, and the speaker they eventually selected turned out to be a diva. On the day of the recording, he showed up late and with a flu. As a result, the recording was unusable. Should I confess to the client what happened? Tell him that everyone else had been difficult and that we had to push back the deadline? At the end of the day, my lack of leadership was to blame. Had I pushed for a decision earlier, we would have been fine. After trying to fix up the botched recording in post production, I grabbed the microphone and spoke the twenty words myself. On the day of the delivery, nobody even commented on the voice over and the commercial aired as planned.

Business Lesson

People need a decision maker. Make bold decisions, even if they are just based on your gut feeling. A good enough solution often works just fine.

Strike the Iron While It's Hot

In Hollywood, things can go into overdrive from one minute to another. You can rise from nothing to a major star almost overnight. People know this, so they make every moment count. When things look up for you in Hollywood, you have to wring the most out of it while you can. When you have the attention of decision makers, this is the moment to fill up your pipeline with projects. Better prepare to have many ideas to strike deals while the iron is still hot. Just as quickly as the opportunity arises, the door may slam shut again. Thinking that you will grab the next chance often proves elusive, as there will simply be no next chance.

The mainstream notion of building success slowly rarely applies to Hollywood. It is true that many stars were unknown longer than they were famous, but there is a tipping point when things accelerate. To take a step back and take a deep breath when the rocket takes off is the wrong strategy. When you see the green light, go at warp speed. Putting your head down and going full steam ahead wins any day. This is of course unsustainable. But in Hollywood, who cares what will happen tomorrow? That is exactly why so many nervous breakdowns and burnouts happen in the business. They seem to be the price of admission.

A manager was pitching his services to me. He said he cared about the long-term careers of his artists who he would slowly build up so they would have a long-term income. "I'm not interested in doing a one-time deal for twenty million for an artist," he explained. "I would rather build a long-term career for them." It was hard for me to follow his logic. When there is an opportunity to strike a twenty-million-dollar deal, why turn it down? Most people believe it is impossible to make a fortune quickly anyway. But virtually all entertainment riches came about in a short time. Earning your keep slowly is the safer bet, but Hollywood runs on a different clock. The short-term future always matters more than anything else.

Business Lesson

When you have the attention of decision makers, strike all the deals you can. As soon as the door opens just a tiny crack, rush right in and take up all the space you can.

Offer On-site Perks to Your Employees and Clients

Some workplaces in Hollywood are truly unique. The offices of some film studios, computer game companies, and advertising agencies are often playgrounds with hammocks and swings, electric scooters, punching bags, and arcade games. Fully stocked kitchens with healthy and unhealthy snacks, refrigerators brimming with cans of soft drinks and microwave meals are the rule. All of this is free, of course. Just like Google's headquarters in Mountain View, some companies offer on-site carwashes, haircuts, and massages. The result is that employees never want go home. How does a shoebox of an apartment compare with such a workplace? Better spend off-work hours on the premises as well. When an idea strikes at ten o'clock at night, the movie editing bay or other workstation is just a few steps away. Will employees come in on the weekend to finish an important client project? With pleasure.

Employees are proud to work for a cool company. They love telling their friends about the perks they get. This can do wonders for the reputation of a company, especially when talent is scarce. Instead of competing for the best and brightest on salary alone, they provide a remarkable work experience that may be worth its weight in gold. The boss makes it seem as if he did a favor to his staff. How can they refuse when he makes demands? Under stress, stored goodwill goes a long way.

The same applies to clients. You want them to look forward to visiting your company. When they can walk in and take a beer from the refrigerator before the meeting, chances are you will keep them for a long time. Clients rarely find a relaxed environment at many of their suppliers. Providing remote-controlled cars and a Playstation often already checks the box for being an extraordinary workplace. Companies can learn how to motivate employees and clients from Hollywood in a big way.

Business Lesson

Gamify the work experience. Offer free coffee, soft drinks, and other perks whenever possible. Clients and employees will be happier, and your company will gain a good reputation that may save you money in the future.

Prepare for Success or It Will Go To Your Head

Whenever you start a project in Hollywood, you naturally imagine that it will be wildly successful. The whole town lives from the dreams of people to become stars despite the fact that it becomes a reality for only a handful. The entertainment industry needs to keep the illusion alive that everyone can make it big. Ironically, even though they are chasing success, it takes most people by surprise when it happens. As a result, unexpected windfalls overwhelm them and they start undoing them as they happen.

In a music project, I witnessed this from the front row. The singer I was developing was fresh out of college. In her early twenties, she had never worked anywhere besides some part-time jobs during school. When she signed a recording contract with a major record label, they paid her an advance of over one hundred thousand dollars. For someone with just a few hundred dollars to her name, this was a shock. Immediately she moved out of her shared apartment and signed a lease for a condo by the beach.

She bought a German sports car and even talked about soon gifting a Bentley ("the one that Paris Hilton drives") to her father. Spending money now had a bigger mind share than working on the music project that the advance had been paid for in the first place. Before the deal, the singer was insecure and worked hard on her voice. Now she was absolutely certain she had nothing more to learn. Needless to say, this project was doomed. If you have ever lived in Los Angeles, you know that money will run through your fingers like sand. Even though it sounds like a lot, six digits will rarely last long. In this case, all of three months. Then the singer was on the brink of personal bankruptcy. The music project was beyond repair and the record label ultimately shut it down.

You may know how of handle money, but also think about the people you work with. They may stop thinking clearly when they have disposable cash. Be careful to select people who will be able to withstand temptation. Otherwise, they may sink your projects as soon as they become profitable.

Business Lesson

Make sure you and your business partners prepare for success. Keep your act together when you draw media attention or earn large sums of money. Unless you are careful, success will disappear as quickly as it came about.

Beware of Burnout

You will experience extreme demands on your energy when a project blows up in Hollywood. After spending years in obscurity laboring away somewhere in a studio apartment, you may find yourself in everybody's favor overnight. Just as you need to prepare yourself to deal with unexpected success and all the benefits it brings, you should also have in mind your health over the longer term.

This is easier said than done. When you have huge opportunities all of a sudden, you should capitalize on them. That is exactly what you worked for all these years, after all. But what good does success do you unless you can fully enjoy it? Everyone in Hollywood had at least one nervous breakdown or burnout. Many struggle with addiction. More than you think have attempted suicide. Most of them are in therapy. Is it worth earning one hundred million dollars and then dropping dead the next year?

In the beginning, it is cool to fly to Tokyo for meetings, stop over in Stockholm for more meetings, and then return in Los Angeles in less than a week. In your private plane with your own bed, your personal assistants, good food, your friends on board, and limousine pickup on the runway, you may be able to circle the globe three times a month. But as long as you travel commercial, it will take a toll. When success hits, people will make demands on you until you either break or push back. If you understand your boundaries early on, it will be easier to manage success in the long run.

Business Lesson

Find a work-life a balance before a crisis forces you to adjust your lifestyle. Reflect on what is important to you beyond making your project or company successful.

Your Impact Could Be Global

Hollywood enjoys a unique position as the entertainment capital of the world. Regardless of where on the globe you are, it is almost impossible to escape its tentacles. I saw reruns of *Friends* on TV in remote areas in Indonesia and installments of *Babylon Five* in the jungle in Thailand. The domination of worldwide entertainment by this town is undeniable.

The fun part is that if you are in Hollywood, it could be you who will produce the next hit song or feature film that will touch people's life wherever in the world they may be. I was watching the news in a small European country, when I heard a song of mine that I had produced in Los Angeles. *Electronic Arts*, a computer game company a stone's throw from my studio, had licensed that song for a game. The news program showed a report about that particular game and my song played in the background. This was only possible because my Hollywood agent knew the Hollywood music supervisor at that particular Hollywood game company. Outsiders rarely have the network that enables such global reach.

The irony of it is that the most mundane tasks were on my mind when I made that song. While I produced it, I literally lived in my studio. For dinner, I would get a takeaway salad from the health food store around the corner. In front of the computer, I would then eat that salad while working on the track. This took forever because the vocal would never sound the way I wanted. On some days, I would work until the sun came up. After closing my eyes for a few hours on the couch, I would pick up from where I left. And a few months later a European reporter bounced up and down to that song on national television.

It was a strange feeling to notice what I produced in my little studio by the beach could end up in the living rooms of millions of people around the world. I felt a responsibility to not let them down and to make sure they got a positive vibe. What people experienced when they listened to my music became more important to me than which exact frequency on the spectrum the bass occupied. At the end of the day, when the content is bad, technology will rarely improve it. When the content is great, technology is just a tool to enhance its impact.

Business Lesson

The project you are working on could reach many more people than you think. Impact and meaning is more important than technical features or minor details that you may waste a lot of time with.

Surround Yourself With Smart People

Being the smartest person in the room is flattering for a while. Nevertheless, it will rarely do you any good to achieve long-term success. Successful people in Hollywood know this. They pride themselves for scouting out the best talent and then have them do the job for them. For film composers, this can be a productive strategy. Once a composer has reached a certain fame, he often hires young and hungry talent to flesh out his ideas. Several people are involved in writing the music that the audience perceives as the work of the genius alone. This is hardly a secret. It is perfectly normal in Hollywood to take credit for the work of others.

Of course this is only possible when your staff, your professional network, and your entourage come up with ideas better than yours. If you want to stay on the cutting edge, you need to have talented people by your side. They will share with you new trends that they spotted, observations and analyses for future opportunities, and introduce their own extended network into yours.

Business Lesson

Unless you are an egomaniac, try to be the dumbest person in the room. Always seek out those who are smarter than you. You will constantly learn and improve this way.

CHAPTER 6: PRODUCTIVITY HACKS

Hollywood gives off the impression that all day long, creative people work on exciting projects and have a lot of fun in the process. While this can happen, laboring on a motion picture or music project is also exhausting, frustrating, and often unglamorous. A lot of work goes into making these products what they are, and most of it is invisible to the consumer. Like anywhere else, you sometimes have to do a job. For this you will need a strong motivation. Productivity hacks can also help you pull through. Here are some that I learned over the years. I still use in my current projects almost daily.

Borrow for Inspiration

Hollywood is well-known for claiming credit for other people's work. Of course you should avoid plagiarism, but you can always draw inspiration from those who walked before you. When writing a film score, music composers often rely on a so-called *temp score*. It consists of pieces of existing film scores that they put in the places of the movie where they imagine a music cue. That temp score roughly follows the same style like the music they want to write. This is often half the rent in writing film music. Composers will write new music, of course. But the overall direction will be similar. I had a vast library of film scores that I would match with the movies I was working on. It was always helpful to have something there for inspiration instead of starting out with a blank page.

In Hollywood, drawing inspiration from existing work is an art form in itself. It can help in many other projects besides film music. Writers have folders with clippings of stories, news articles, and other bits they can sift through to seek inspiration. Directors do the same with movie scenes they collect that they like for light, camera angle, color, or anything else. Nobody needs to know where your inspiration came from. Building on existing creative work in a smart way can save you a lot of time.

Business Lesson

Collect material that inspires you. When you have a creative block, look through your library for ideas. This beats staring at a blank page and trying to come up with something completely original.

Take Breaks

My office was opposite *Gold's Gym* in Venice, two blocks from the beach. Whenever you see a ridiculously huge bodybuilder in a movie, chances are they work out in that gym. The place is a landmark in Los Angeles, an open plan building with hundreds of fitness machines. Actors, some pop stars, and other celebrities also train there. When I felt I had to take a break and a change of scenery, I would shuffle across the street and work out for half an hour. It was refreshing to get some distance between myself and whatever project I was working on. The place was always good for an interesting chat as well. You never knew who you would meet. When I got back to the studio, I would usually have new ideas that quickly moved the projects along.

Some film studios have basketball hoops in their courtyards. Others have trampolines or electro scooters to zip around the neighborhood. People in Hollywood make use of these facilities. Friends of mine went surfing for the same purpose. Or they went to the massage place for a Thai massage. When you need a fresh perspective, get out of the office and do something completely different. By this I mean more than just going to the cafeteria or the parking lot for a smoke. Physically leave the building and do something different for half an hour. Then resume where you left off with fresh energy.

Business Lesson

You can push only for so long before you need to recharge. Take breaks from time to time to put some distance between you and your work. A brisk physical activity usually works best.

Finish the Job

Thousands of people in Hollywood are laboring endlessly on their scripts, their novels, their ideas for TV shows, and other ambitious and not so ambitious projects. If they ever leave the idea stage, most of them take years to reach a level of near completion. Then they often linger in a loop of indecisive revision. I am talking about those projects that the barman/writer and the waitress/actress have in their drawers. They may be good, but what sets them apart from professional projects is that they always remain incomplete. Only few projects in Hollywood ever get finished.

This is a great advantage to you. If all you do is finish your project, you are already ahead of the pack. So if you produce a music album, write a comedy, or come up with anything else that you can show in a professional setting, you are a winner. Having a product alone signals to the industry that you are a finisher.

What would you prefer: A brilliant idea and never completing the project, or a good idea and completing it within time and budget? You already know the answer. Finished your work and present it even though you may believe your ideas need further improvement. Just collect feedback and then improve later. Show something good that is done and you are on the path to success.

Business Lesson

Better show something decent that is finished than a genius idea that is incomplete. As long as your project includes everything necessary to move to the next level, you are already ahead.

Just Ten More Minutes

When I am exhausted and just about had it with a project, I often reach over to the kitchen timer. I set it for ten minutes and then give the project my full attention until the alarm goes off. This exercise is powerful. It will focus your thinking and assure you that after ten minutes, you can let it all go. This productivity hack can give you a quick boost when you need to come up with an idea or reach a milestone. Your best work might happen then and there.

Especially in creative work, we often think that we need divine inspiration to come up with anything original. Sure, that is a big part of it, too. But forcing your brain to think harder and tap into those hidden reserve can be like magic fairy dust. What I produced with this technique often surprised me. There are projects where close to eighty percent of my good ideas sprung from these last ten minutes. Just try it and see if it works.

Business Lesson

When you feel stuck in a project, set a timer for ten minutes and force yourself to come forward with ideas until the alarm goes off. This concentrates your energy and lets you off the hook when the time is up.

Avoid Energy Drain

Instead of constantly recharging your batteries also check what drains your energy. You may find that you need to avoid doing certain things before you add more firepower. This may be the smart phone going off every few minutes. Or the window with Twitter messages on your computer screen. When you need focus, first stop interrupting yourself. After all, it is you who controls your environment.

People can also zap our energy. I was auditioning singers for the title credits of a movie. One singer was unable to make it to the main audition and asked if she could come in the next morning for fifteen minutes to record a short sample. She did an OK job in the recording booth, but then started letting me know her life story. How she had to escape her small town in some farm to state to express herself creatively. How she was looking for a "benefactor" to help her with her money woes. How she considered more plastic surgery because all the other girls she knew had it. She was a pro in keeping the conversation going and making it hard to stop. After one hour or so, I finally complimented her out the door. It was impossible to do any work for half the day after that. A dark air was hanging in the studio, and only a long walk by the ocean restored my energy. Since then, I paid more attention and cut situations off that had the risk of zapping energy.

Business Lesson

Avoid anything that is draining your energy. This may be disruption by digital toys or people with a negative attitude. No need to be polite about this. If a situation drains you, stop it.

CHAPTER 7: HOW TO SPOT AND AVOID TROUBLE

In Hollywood, few projects will go all smoothly. They may start promising and then unexpectedly turn sour. Others may already have red flags coming up right at the beginning. Because you need to make your time and energy count, better learn how to spot them as early as possible. Spotting and avoiding trouble is an essential skill, one that I wish I had paid more attention to earlier. Through trial and error, I realized which signs foreshadowed trouble later down the road. Others set off the alarm bells ringing right of the beginning. You will save yourself and others much grief when you become sensitive to these signals. This chapter explains some of them.

Separate Business And Pleasure

A director may cast his own girlfriend for a movie. A music producer may choose a singer he would like to go out with, even though others fit the project better. An aspiring actress believes that "sex sells," so she tries to attract her first movie roles this way. Such things certainly happen in Hollywood. Even though many people blur the line between their work and their private life, this often leads to unnecessary trouble.

Those who work on high-profile projects rarely cross that line. They avoid anything that can complicate and delay projects. It is their time and money at stake, along with the capital of shareholders and other parties. If you let them down and sink an important project, you may never work in this town again. Why take unnecessary risks? Stay away from anything with a high probability of landing you in court or in jail.

It is easy to spot trouble in Hollywood with this filter. When people hit on anyone who walks into their office, they are seldom of the sort that will last long. The same goes for those who need to "take their vitamins" every half hour. Sure, there are exceptions. But they are few and far between. Better be professional and keep business and your private life separate. Only work with those who have the same standards in their own careers.

Business Lesson

Separate personal relationships and romance from your professional projects. Avoid taking risks, especially with third-party capital. Stay away from those who blur the line. They will attract unnecessary complications sooner or later.

Too Good to Be True

Next to those who want to make their mark with creative skills and projects, Hollywood also attracts people who feel they get a second chance after they exhausted their credit elsewhere. After all, most jobs in the entertainment business rarely need a professional qualification or experience to get started. A big pool like Hollywood, where thousands of hopefuls come and go each week to strike it rich, attracts many shady characters. They view it like playing the lottery. Sooner or later, they will hit the jackpot. Unfortunately, often to the disadvantage of others. We have all seen deals that are too good to be true. Better stay away from this crowd.

A neighbor I had known for a while had cooked up a story about some Texan relatives who owned an oil field in Nigeria. They allegedly needed to raise two hundred thousand dollars to pay off the authorities to release blocked funds. They just needed five thousand dollars more, and then they could finally unfreeze that account. If I could just lend him the five thousand, he would pay me back a million, which could be as early as next week. A return of twenty thousand percent in a week? Does this sound plausible? But mind you, in Hollywood, skilled actors can pull off any story convincingly. The sad thing is, more people than you think fall for these scams.

Too good to be true is about more than money. When a director promises you that you will be the lead composer on a major feature film if you can only score his trailer for free, how can you be sure of it? If he finds someone bankrolling his movie, do you believe he will stick out his neck for you? The same also applies to unassuming actors and actresses who believe that being friends with benefits with directors and producers will land big acting roles for them. Most of these deals are too good to be true. Those who are really in power are more professional than making impossible promises. Just use common sense.

Business Lesson

When something sounds too good to be true, it usually is. Some people will make a convincing case why their project is different. Just use common sense, and the truth will become obvious.

This Time Is Never Different

I was interviewing assistants to work in my studio. Most of them made a good impression and were professional, but one of them offered up a memorable learning experience. After she had explained her resume, I asked about references to previous employers. Her face immediately darkened. It turned out that she had sued her previous boss because he had not paid her the last salary. This can happen, and there is nothing wrong with sticking up for your rights, even if it means taking the matter up in small claims court. But she would go on about how horrible it had been working there, the uninspiring chores she had to do there, how everybody was mean to her, and how she eventually got fired. When I asked her about other experiences, it turned out that it had been no different in her previous job. She hated it, thought everybody there was stupid, got fired, and then sued her boss. Incredible, I thought. How does she expect me to hire her after what she just told me?

Hollywood has a short memory. You are only as good as your last project. The excellent work you did ten projects ago is unimportant, especially if your last one failed epically. If someone piles failure upon failure, then chances are that the unlucky streak will continue. Unless there is a concerted effort to turn things around, things rarely change by themselves. I should have checked people's track record earlier. Once I started, I was amazed how much information came to light that was a clear deal breakers.

Business Lesson

Before you work with people, check their track record. Unless they have good explanations for gaps and flaws, things will be rarely be different this time.

Airhead Alert

Just as movies portray a fantasy world with superheroes and happy endings, Hollywood itself is all about make-believe. This goes so deep that some people have stopped to notice when they are acting. Fiction and reality is a blur to them. As a result, ninety-nine percent of what people tell you in Hollywood will never happen. It is largely wishful thinking.

If someone proclaims that they are great friends with celebrity so and so, who will surely get behind a project and push it on the big screen, he may have never seen that celebrity in real life. If someone takes credit for producing this song or that movie, they may have never been on the set. It is a movie playing in their head. This archetype is similar to the wannabe we met earlier. Wannabes are actually trying to get themselves off the ground, but with mediocre efforts and flawed strategy. Airheads are making everything up. Instead of doing something, they *think* they do it and fail to distinguish between their thoughts and reality. This may sound very strange, and it is. Many airheads walk the streets in Hollywood, and they are often borderline schizophrenic.

You will meet people with a Beverly Hills address who roll up in expensive British sports cars. Later you will find out they live in their ex-girlfriends' apartments and cannot make the next car payment. Appearances can unduly impress. They are often smoke and mirrors. The same goes for the business advice they give you or the industry contacts they supposedly have. Take everything with a grain of salt, and feel free to ask them to explain and back up their claims. Use *Six Sigma* on them and ask them the *five whys*, a series of five questions that drill down on how a situation came about. You will see immediately from their reactions if they are for real. If they hesitate or contradict themselves, they are an airhead.

When people have something to hide, they are often in a great hurry. Everything needs to happen yesterday. By rushing things, they try to gloss over the fact that their projects are half-baked. They may also be flying by the seat of their pants, making things up as they go. If you are serious about your business, avoid this group. Better focus your energy on those with a solid reputation who can make things happen for you in a professional way.

Business Lesson

As soon as you notice some discrepancy between what people try to project and what you read between the lines, stop. When they try to hurry you along, perhaps with even more outrageous promises, better run.

If You Lie Down With Dogs, You Will Get Up With Fleas

It is obvious that you should avoid mingling with those who have a bad reputation or conduct shady business. In Hollywood, however, many believe that a certain degree of shadiness is necessary to do business. Like in a banana republic, where bribes and corruption are commonplace, they believe that Hollywood demands a toll on ethics and good conscience. I disagree. In all my time there, I never felt I had to do something I would regret later to reach a certain goal. Much of this has to do with the company you keep. Their influence is much bigger than you think. Make sure your value system stays intact, and keep on screening new people you meet to see if they match with your style.

Many celebrities have a reputation for being bad boys or bad girls, trashing hotel rooms, making big scenes at public events, and getting DUIs. Some of this may be true, but it is often all a big publicity stunt. When you meet them personally, they turn out to be focused business professionals who even admit that their press personality is a marketing strategy. Being famous is a business that takes work to run. It demand focus and energy and leaves little room for self-destructive behavior. Unfortunately, non-celebrities who start imitating those press stories quickly spiral downwards. They attract mostly unprofessional wannabes and adopt nasty habits by osmosis. If you want to make it in Hollywood, I recommend you stay clean. If you lie down with dogs, you will get up with fleas.

Business Lesson

Make sure those you do business with live up to your own professional and ethical standards. If a business deal made you uncomfortable in your hometown, then also avoid it in Hollywood.

If Something Is On A Whole New Level, It Is Sure To Fail

There is a lot of music production going on in Hollywood besides film music. Most of the top 40 pop songs that play on the radio emerged from a recording studio there. Music is an interesting business. You can write and produce a song in a day that can become a hit all around the world and will pay royalties for a decade. Because you can make an impact with music faster than with a movie or book, success goes to people's head faster. Most of the negative gossip in the media has to do with musicians, after all. It is common to hear in the industry that this or that song will be a "game changer" or "the next big thing." This is often a result of an inflated ego and has little to do with the quality of the music. When people lose touch with reality, they are prone to make mistakes or act silly in other ways. This will quickly sink any project.

Whenever someone told me that their song or album would be "on a whole new level," I knew instantly that the opposite would be the case. It would disappear in obscurity before it could unleash its "world domination" on the unsuspecting audience. But you need extreme self-confidence to become successful, I hear you say. It is true that those who have good self-esteem are more likely to act on their beliefs. However, pep talks in the style of "You can do it" mostly inflate people's egos. They do little for extraordinary performance. Even with big stars, those projects with a radical impact always started in humble and unglamorous ways. Successful professionals just put their head down and finish their work. They have no need to convince everybody with inflated statements that their art is great. When they hear the result, they will know by themselves.

Business Lesson

Beware of statements like "on a whole new level," "a game changer," or "the next big thing." Hyping things will do you a disfavor. Successful projects start unassumingly. Better do the best work you can and then let your clients decide.

CHAPTER 8: DAMAGE CONTROL OR HOW TO TAKE THE HEAT

More of my Hollywood projects failed than were successful. There is profound learning in failures, and I should have taken the time earlier to analyze what exactly went wrong to save the situation the next time around. Much of it has to do with avoiding sticky situations in the first place. We learned about how to do this in the chapter about spotting and avoiding trouble. Here we will learn about what Hollywood does when the house is already on fire.

Avoid Panic, Stay Positive

The three musketeers were riding their horses through a tavern in a movie I was watching in a Hollywood theatre. I was impressed with the deep bass that the sound designer had mixed into the noise of the hooves clacking on the wooden tables, until I noticed that the sound came from somewhere else. This was an earthquake. If you have never been in one, it will surprise you that they are very loud. You hear a booming rumble for a few seconds, and then the vibrations start. Everybody in the theatre was screaming, the screen went black, and we were all ducking behind the chairs. After a few seconds, it was over. "Uhm, you guys all OK?" a voice from the projection room inquired. Everybody was laughing. The film started up again, and things returned to normal in less than a minute. Nobody left the theatre, and it was all forgotten by the end of the movie.

We all know that Los Angeles lies on a major fault line that is prone to earthquakes. Regardless, people in Hollywood prefer to watch a movie than worry about an earthquake. Why panic if there is no real danger?

Business Lesson

When disaster strikes, a positive attitude goes a long way. Avoid panic, take a deep breath, and then assess the situation with a clear head.

Always Wait A Day Before Sending An Angry Response

Some people and situations in Hollywood will inevitably infuriate you beyond measure. Somebody may have affirmed to you that they have the credentials to pull off a certain business deal. You invested, and now they got themselves arrested on fraud charges. Or you may have worked on a project for years, only to find your business partner and his lawyer tried to write you out of a million-dollar contract that was to be signed today. Anger is a natural emotion. Suppressing it is unhealthy. However, incensed reactions can haunt you later. They may destroy a reputation that took years to build in a few seconds.

When you are upset, take a step back and let it cool off before you do anything. In fact, you should always wait at least one day before you respond to anything critical, whether good or bad. When you are angry, type all the terrible things you want to tell that person, but avoid hitting send until later. The next day, you will often slap your forehead and thank yourself for delaying your reaction. In digital communications, you should remain polite. People do show around silly emails they receive. There are flame wars going on right now, often over nothing. Why waste your time, let alone put your professional network at risk? Always cool your temper before you react to unpleasant situations.

Business Lesson

Email, texts, and messages are out there forever. Draft angry answers, but avoid sending them before waiting at least one day. Stay polite and detached in all your digital communications. When you have to level with someone, do it offline and off the record.

Suspend Work At The First Sign Of Trouble

My first big Hollywood project was an electronic pop album. The manager who had given me the job was an energetic Jack of all trades. He was grooming a young singer to become a pop star. This actually happened, but years later, after changing her name, and under new management. The project I was working on was her first professional music project.

Entertainment business is like launching startups. Someone has a good idea that attracts investors. He then sets up a company in which all those involved own shares, based on the value they bring to the table. In this particular project, the investor was a burly businessman from the Midwest.

He had caught the Hollywood bug and wanted to start a career as a financier. He and the manager got on fabulously, at the beginning. Halfway into the project, problems began to surface. There was no paperwork and they had neglected to iron out who would be the principal decision maker. Naturally, both claimed ownership. I had started work on a handshake agreement with the manager (big mistake), but it was the financier who had signed the check. Because he funded it, he had creative control of the album, he reasoned. The manager made an equally convincing point. He was in charge since he had put the whole thing together. It was a mess.

I asked a friend what to do in this situation. He advised me to suspend all work and give the same answer to both the manager and the financier. "Just tell them you're busy with other projects until they pay the remainder of your fee and they both sign an agreement that outlines ownership," he advised. The next morning, I was lifting weights in the gym when the phone rang. It was the financier. After a few minutes of chit-chat, he started trying to convince me that he owned the project and that I should from now on work with him directly. I gave him the canned answer. One minute later, the manager was calling. We should work together without the financier from now on, he proposed. He also got the canned answer. They had no other choice than reaching an agreement. A few days later, the were reunited at the recording studio as if nothing had happened. Work resumed and the album soon wrapped.

Stopping all work until others have resolved their issues has worked well for me since. I used this strategy when people missed payments and in any kind of contract disputes. It is important to stay neutral. Once things go back to normal, act as if nothing had happened. That is the Hollywood way.

Business Lesson

At the first sign of problems, suspend work on the project until the air clears. Avoid taking sides. Things will often work themselves out if you stay neutral.

Get Up On Your Feet Right Away

Of course, we wish that all of our projects are successful. After all, this is the fuel that keeps us going. In most business projects the odds of success are in your favor, but Hollywood is different. If you are lucky, you have perhaps a one-percent chance of striking it rich. Regardless, all the screenwriters, aspiring actors, singers, and other adventurers in Los Angeles get up every morning and labor on their vision with renewed energy. They have gotten used to rejection, and use it as a driving force to keep going. After all, if you can rack up one hundred rejections with a project, the odds that the next person will say yes are much higher.

Business Lesson

A big part of success is refusing to give up. When someone turns down your project, keep your spirits high. Improve the odds of success by getting up on your feet quickly after each rejection or failure and charge forward.

Stay Out of the Blame Game

Something can always go wrong in a project. When tempers are flying high, it is easy to point fingers and blame others for the mistakes they made. However, the most successful people avoid this. I was producing the music for an image film for a five-star hotel chain. The movie was fifteen minutes long, and the production had taken months. Since it was a high-profile project, the client made decisions by committee. Everyone working on the project convened by conference call once a week. When you see people face to face, music is already a difficult thing to speak about. But when their suggestions come out of a speaker phone, it is all the more complicated.

The film finally wrapped, and the final presentation was scheduled for the next day. I went to my favorite restaurant for lunch right after the director had picked up the CD with the audio files and turned off the phone. When I returned an hour later, he was standing in front of the door ringing his hands. It turned out I had given him an empty CD by mistake. He had noticed it when he tried to align the music with the film together with his editor. How embarrassing. He had every right to be furious. Nonetheless, it surprised me how lightly he took the problem, given the size of the project, the budget involved, and the looming deadline. We quickly cleared up the issue in the most positive way possible. Not once did he make a negative remark about my blunder, but he stressed that he should have paid more attention when he accepted the CD. His upbeat attitude impressed me, and it is no surprise why he went on to produce many other high-profile projects afterwards.

Business Lesson

When things go wrong, refrain from blaming others for their mistake.
If necessary, take responsibility yourself for the blunders of others.
This will give you credit and establish you as the leader in the eyes of
your clients.

Take The High Road

After a few years of running my recording studio, a project of mine had turned into a surprise hit. It got worldwide media coverage and offers for record deals from major record labels. At the same time, it became clear that the manager I started out with was a less than perfect fit for the project, and I began looking for a better business partner.

One person I interviewed for the job turned out to be a real nuisance. Since a decent amount of money was in the record deal, he tried to grab a share of it through subterfuge. After the two short meetings he had with me, he claimed he had given me business advice that would entitle him to twenty percent of the next payment from the recording contract. He made an effort to intimidate me, and threatened legal action. He would call my office, shouting abuses on the answering machine. In some of his emails, one in five words were expletives. All in all, the guy was a genuine Hollywood dirt bag.

If you have ever experienced anything like this, you know how this can grind you down and suck every ounce of energy out of you. You want to react emotionally, and lash out at the people who are clearly in the wrong. But as soon as you do that, they have you right where they want you. They will mince your words and may even find grounds to sue you for something minor you wrote in one of those angry emails you sent off in an act of blind fury. The best strategy by far is to take the high road. What do I mean by that? Simply ignore any of the verbal abuses and let the situation wash over you. Avoid direct confrontation at all cost. Never negotiate with terrorists. Focus on positive things and let the issue resolve itself.

Fraudsters will have other targets besides you. They work on several projects at the same time, hoping that one of them will become profitable. When you stop being a target by completely deflating the matter they try to nail you with, they will have to focus their attention elsewhere. After they have been silent for a few weeks, consider the matter closed. The same goes for anything else you wish to avoid in your life. Completely ignore it until it goes away. That is how Hollywood deals with problems.

Business Lesson

When others try to entangle you in a legal dispute out of fraudulent motives, take the high road. Avoid all contact, ignore their requests, and let the issue resolve itself.

Never Burn The Bridges

I met hundreds of people during my seven years in Hollywood. Some of them are great friends to this day, others I am happy to never see again. Still, it is possible that they will cross my path again. They may even call the shots on a project I take part in. When that happens, we wish that we could turn back the clock and make things right. Perhaps we would avoid that angry email that badmouthed them to others, or the blog where we posted something silly they did or said. We should be aware that we may rely on someone's good graces again in the future.

In Hollywood, keeping the connection is crucial. Sure, many people have personal feuds with others. They may even publicly humiliate each other or engage in flame wars, for everyone to see. Who gains anything from this? When you have dropped a nuclear bomb, it is very difficult to make up again. Better avoid anything you may have to undo later. If there is a slight chance that you may work together again, this is a small price to pay.

Business Lesson

Even when others disappoint you, never burn the bridge. If there is a slight possibility that you will work together again, you should be at least on speaking terms. Why destroy relationships that you may need to reactivate later?

CHAPTER 9: MY MAIN TAKEAWAYS

I learned a lot from my Hollywood years where things were often far from smooth and enjoyable. Even though all the business lessons in this book are useful for the consulting work I am doing today, some of them stand out. They span more than one category because they combine several of the strategies we examined earlier. This chapter describes my most important takeaways.

The Show Must Go On

On the surface, most people in Los Angeles seem happy. They appear to be having fun doing whatever they do. They must be living their dream. Achieving that dream, however, demands a lot. You need to be very good at what you do, and you must have most of the business skills we examined in this book. You need to deal with uncertainty, unpleasant situations, and high tension. And on top of that, all of it should look effortless and natural.

Even when everything goes wrong in a project, you still need to deliver. As soon as you start complaining or become difficult yourself, you have lost. Nobody cares about your troubles, only results matter. When things look darkest, that is when you put on your best smile and give your best performance. Just as the show must go on outwardly, you must also motivate yourself to keep going. All problems will eventually solve themselves.

Most projects are seldom either black or white, either a failure or a success. But occasionally, disaster will strike. If nothing takes you by surprise and you can cope even with extreme demands, then you have a huge advantage. As soon as I learned that, I felt I could master any situation.

Business Lesson

Just as the show must go on outwardly, you also need to motivate yourself to keep going. When things look dark, put on your best smile and charge ahead. All problems will eventually solve themselves.

Up Your Game

When I look back on the time before I had worked in Hollywood, I am a little embarrassed. I ran my business similar to others, but compared to what I did in Los Angeles, most of it seems like driving a sports car in second gear. The main difference before and after lies in my ability to cope with difficult situations. I had regularly complained when I was still in my office at eight o'clock at night. In Hollywood, working for seventy-two hours straight was a normal occurrence. In every respect, my projects became bigger, better, more challenging, and more fulfilling. It was helpful to find out that more was possible. I started to think bigger and knew that I could live up to the high standards I had set for myself.

No one seeks out sticky situations on purpose or particularly likes to work under extremely demanding circumstances. But when I learned to deal with high tension, I started to set the bar for my business higher. When I left Los Angeles after seven years, I noticed once more that most businesses in the rest of the world are far from operating at full potential. They think they are, but I doubt they would last long when the heat is turned up.

Business Lesson

Being successful is seldom smooth sailing. When you commit to making your mark, set higher demands for yourself. Improve your business skills, your work ethic, your requirements on employees, and your expectations from clients. You will be surprised what is possible.

How You Perceive Others, They Perceive You

Since my office was across the street from one of the most famous gyms in the world, it was natural that I was a regular there. I had several personal trainers over the years and took weightlifting fairly serious at times. I rarely went to the gym every day, but at least three times a week, usually for brief sessions to clear my head.

Towards the end of my seven Hollywood years, I remember a cardio workout on a StairMaster that overlooked the entire gym. My glance wandered from workstation to workstation, and it dawned on me that almost every time I came to the gym, I saw the same faces. What are these people doing, I wondered? Have they nothing else to do? I even felt a little sorry for them. They seemed unchanged in all the seven years that I had been observing them. It looked to me like their life went nowhere. Then it hit me like a ton of bricks. They also had eyes in their head, so they saw me as well. They might ask themselves the same questions. "What's this guy doing here all the time in the middle of the afternoon? Seems he's walking to stand still on his StairMaster there." Whether anyone really cared is another question. I still felt that they were right in a way.

Subconsciously, something shifted in my mind in the next few weeks. Three months later I wound down my recording studio, moved out of my apartment, sold all of my belongings, and left the United States. The time had come to move on.

Business Lesson

Just as you form an opinion about others, they do the same with you. You may come across differently than how you perceive yourself. Put yourself in the shoes of others and imagine how they see you. This can be an eye-opener.

EPILOGUE : BEYOND HOLLYWOOD

Congratulations, you made it through this book. Even though it is about business lessons, they turned out to be very personal. Now you know almost everything about me and my time in Los Angeles. I told you how I think and look at the experiences I collected in that strange place. Hopefully, some of the ideas in this book resonate with you. Both for your business and your personal projects.

No doubt, Hollywood is extreme. As a result, some of the business lessons may seem over the top. But taking them all at face value would miss the point. Perhaps you can tweak them a little or use them as starting points to brainstorm new approaches on your own. In any event, they are unconventional. Whether you work in a creative field or in a more traditional line of business, they may give you a special angle that is hard to find in the traditional business literature. Dealing with your coworkers, bosses, employees, and clients Hollywood-style may introduce a breath of fresh air in your professional network and relationships. When you need ideas to master challenges, you may find them by flipping through this book as well.

Hollywood is also all about diversity. What I learned there differs from what anybody else may have discovered. The same applies to my interpretations. I encourage you to develop them further and compare them with your own observations. Just like a movie can have different meanings for different audiences, I hope you come up with your own takeaways.

How we do something is often more important than *what* we do. As with any business advice, the only thing that matters is how you apply the business lessons from Hollywood. First and foremost, I wanted to inspire you to reflect on things in a different light. If you go out and test something you have read here, I have achieved my goal.

THE END

ABOUT THE AUTHOR

Atom Alex Helling is an entrepreneur, traveler and observer with an unconventional story. He founded companies in Europe, America and Asia, wrote film scores with the best and pop songs for the worst. While living in Los Angeles, he struck a seven-figure deal with a major record label, won several songwriting competitions and produced a documentary about Japanese manga and anime. Then he moved to Tokyo where he started another venture and lived through a 9.0 earthquake. He is still a songwriter and movie enthusiast. And he is also writing about all of the above.

www.atomalex.com

THANK YOU

Before you go, I would like to say "thank you" for purchasing my book. It has been a lot of fun to write, and I hope it was fun to read as well.

Now I would like ask for a small favor. If you enjoyed this book, would you please take a minute or two and leave a review on Amazon. This feedback will help me continue to write the kind of books that entertain and help you get results. And if you loved it, then please let me know. I look forward to hearing from you.

STAY IN TOUCH

To stay in the loop about upcoming books and specials, please sign up for my mailing list on **www.atomalex.com/newsletter**. I am always offering free (or deeply discounted) books to my list. And as a subscriber, you will be the first to know about these special deals.

I look forward to hearing from you. If you have any questions or comments, please reach out to me in any of the following ways:

Website:	www.atomalex.com
Email:	contact@atomalex.com
Twitter:	@atomalexhelling
Facebook:	www.facebook.com/pages/Atom-Alex-Helling/340442666122299

MORE BOOKS BY ATOM ALEX HELLING

Business Lessons from Japan: What I Learned as an Entrepreneur from Samurai, Sushi Chefs, and Earthquakes

This is the second book in the "Business Lessons" series. It explains how readers can use the business strategies of the Japanese, no matter what their line of work or where they are in the world. The author, a media entrepreneur and business consultant, has been working in Tokyo for three years. He breaks down his adventures into eighty-five business lessons that anyone can use in their work and life.

Stories in the book include how the author started and sank a joint venture with a multinational in Tokyo, how he ended up playing Russian roulette eating Japanese blowfish, how he managed to appear like a humble genius, or how he turned down a deal with the yakuza. Each short story concludes with the business lesson the author learned from it and explains how it can help readers solve particular challenges.

www.atomalex.com/business-lessons-japan

www.ingramcontent.com/pod-product-compliance
Lightning Source LLC
Chambersburg PA
CBHW071242170526
45165CB00003B/1204